GLOBAL FINANCE

Sara Miller McCune founded SAGE Publishing in 1965 to support the dissemination of usable knowledge and educate a global community. SAGE publishes more than 1000 journals and over 800 new books each year, spanning a wide range of subject areas. Our growing selection of library products includes archives, data, case studies and video. SAGE remains majority owned by our founder and after her lifetime will become owned by a charitable trust that secures the company's continued independence.

Los Angeles | London | New Delhi | Singapore | Washington DC | Melbourne

GLOBAL FINANCE

PLACES, SPACES AND PEOPLE

SARAH HALL

Los Angeles | London | New Delhi
Singapore | Washington DC | Melbourne

Los Angeles | London | New Delhi
Singapore | Washington DC | Melbourne

SAGE Publications Ltd
1 Oliver's Yard
55 City Road
London EC1Y 1SP

SAGE Publications Inc.
2455 Teller Road
Thousand Oaks, California 91320

SAGE Publications India Pvt Ltd
B 1/I 1 Mohan Cooperative Industrial Area
Mathura Road
New Delhi 110 044

SAGE Publications Asia-Pacific Pte Ltd
3 Church Street
#10-04 Samsung Hub
Singapore 049483

Editor: Robert Rojek
Editorial assistant: Catriona McMullen and
    Matt Oldfield
Production editor: Katherine Haw
Copyeditor: Neville Hankins
Indexer: Judith Lavender
Marketing manager: Susheel Gokarakonda
Cover design: Stephanie Guyaz
Typeset by: C&M Digitals (P) Ltd, Chennai, India
Printed in the UK

Library of Congress Control Number: 2016960007

British Library Cataloguing in Publication data

A catalogue record for this book is available from
the British Library

ISBN 978-1-4739-0593-1
ISBN 978-1-4739-0594-8 (pbk)

At SAGE we take sustainability seriously. Most of our products are printed in the UK using FSC papers and boards.
When we print overseas we ensure sustainable papers are used as measured by the PREPS grading system.
We undertake an annual audit to monitor our sustainability.

'In this rich and compelling text, Sarah Hall delves into the evolution of the financial services industry since the 2008 financial crisis. The narrative is systematic and embedded in the history of the Bretton Wood's era, providing a thorough introduction to the world of finance for students and general audiences. At the same time, Hall's skilful analysis of contemporary "spaces" and "subjects" provides new insight into the cultural economy of global finance and will appeal to scholars and practitioners of finance alike.'

Janelle Knox-Hayes, Professor of Economic Geography and Planning, MIT

'Sarah Hall's indispensable text illuminates the places, spaces and people of global finance. It explores established and emerging banking centres, the shadowy worlds of offshore havens and the daily enmeshment of almost everyone into the complexities of financial markets. Grounded in a cutting-edge reading of critical cultural economy, the book will be a major point of reference for students and scholars of global finance who are dissatisfied with the complacent, uncritical, Anglocentric and mathematics-driven accounts that dominate the disciplines of economics and finance.'

Leo McCann, Professor of Organisation Studies, Alliance Manchester Business School, University of Manchester

'More than ever, individuals, households and firms across the globe now have become entangled into global financial networks: as producers and consumers, financial elites and financial subjects. This book by Sarah Hall convincingly shows how the financial system – far from being a placeless space of monetary flows – is made and transformed in established and new financial centres, and illustrates the consequences experienced by different groups of people and in different places included in or excluded from the system.

With *Global Finance*, Sarah Hall has produced an excellent and comprehensive, long overdue account of financial market-making and increasingly financialised "real" economies. This book – grounded in a critical cultural economy approach – provides a masterful and rich analysis of the places, spaces and people that (re-) produce global financial networks and those that are affected by their operations in variegated ways. It should be essential reading for any student and academic interested in the geographies of finance, but will also appeal to a much broader audience interested in how the modern, financialised economy and its (il)logics came about and the ways in which it impacts on the everyday lives of people across the world.'

Martin Hess, Senior Lecturer in Human Geography, University of Manchester

'The world of finance continues to be a dynamic and rapidly changing institutional and spatial environment. This book is a state-of-the-art and fascinating analysis of the locational and relational geography of finance and its associated markets, networks and centres. It offers a contemporary and forward looking critique that will be of relevance to all those with an interest in global finance.'

Robert Huggins, Professor of Economic Geography, Cardiff University

'An insightful exposition and sympathetic critique of the cultural economy approach to finance, demonstrating clearly how places, spaces and people matter in the production and reproduction of global financial markets. Richly illustrated and clearly structured, it should be a great resource for students and scholars of financial geography and finance in general. Financial Geography has been waiting for a single-authored, accessible textbook-like work for a long time!'

Dariusz Wójcik, Professor of Economic Geography, Oxford University and Chair of the Global Network on Financial Geography www.fingeo.net

'Sarah Hall's *Global Finance* is an outstanding guide through the world of financial centres, capital flows and financial elites. Using a cultural economy approach, Hall succeeds in laying barre what has remained hidden for even the best-informed insiders.

In the first part of her book, she uses a political economy lens to describe the transformations in global finance after the demise of the Bretton Woods settlement. The second part focuses on the remaining importance of place even in an age of digitalized finance. Through discussions of how London has reproduced its top position, how Singapore and Hong Kong have wriggled their way into the top spots and how offshore centres have changed their outlook in response to new regulation, the new discipline of financial geography is shown to be a crucial part of global finance. The third part finally zooms in on the importance of elites for the production and reproduction of global finance. Next to a discussion of the infrastructure needed for the making of financial elites, Hall also zooms in on the production of financial subjects among the mass of consumers of financial products as well as how this reproduces and furthers existing socio-economic inequalities.

All in all, Hall has succeeded in bringing together state of the art research to open up an empirical field which, as the 2008 financial crisis has amply demonstrated, is way too important to leave to insiders. Given its clarity and its sophistication, I hope this book will become a crucial textbook for the training of the next generation of financial geographers.'

Ewald Engelen, Professor of Financial Geography, University of Amsterdam

'The economic crisis of 2007 has moved finance to the centre of social science. Firmly embedded within a cultural economy approach, Sarah Hall discusses the spaces of finance and how they affect different places and the people who live there in this superbly researched book.'

Manuel B. Aalbers, Associate Professor of Human Geography, KU Leuven

'For critical geographers, economists, and other heterodox social scientists alike, Sarah Hall has done us all a great service. She has brought together a vast literature on the cultural and social dimensions of the global financial system and, most importantly, revealed its core theme – the rapidly changing "spaces of post-crisis global finance". Theoretically astute and amply illustrated with examples from different levels of the hierarchy of the financial system, *Global Finance* is at once sympathetic critique and significant extension of the literature on the political economy of money and finance. In this wide-ranging synthesis, Hall coalesces a close reading of a wide array of new thinking on a twenty-first century cultural economy approach to money and finance. Her book provides a penetrating analysis that transcends the disciplinary divisions that for too long have obscured a unified understanding of the origins of finance-led capitalism beyond the political fragmentation that underpins the regulatory and institutional landscapes of its financial centres.'

David Bieri, Associate Professor of Public Policy and Real Estate Faculty Fellow, School of Public & International Affairs, Virginia Tech

CONTENTS

LIST OF FIGURES

LIST OF TABLES

ABOUT THE AUTHOR

Sarah Hall is Professor of Economic Geography at the University of Nottingham, having been educated at the Universities of Cambridge and Bristol. Her work focuses on advancing cultural economy approaches to understandings of markets, power and elites under conditions of finance-led capitalism. Supported by funding from the Economic and Social Research Council, the British Academy, the Leverhulme Trust and the Nuffield Foundation, her research mostly centres on London's international financial district and its relations with North America, Europe and, increasingly, China. Her work has been published in a number of leading academic journals. She was appointed an Editor of the journal *Geoforum* in 2013 and held a British Academy Mid-Career Fellowship in 2015–2017.

ACKNOWLEDGEMENTS

This project, and the wider research on which it builds, has benefited hugely from the support of a number of friends, colleagues and family. I would like formally to acknowledge the support of the ESRC (RES-061-25-0071) and the British Academy (MD130065) who each funded two major research projects which gave me the time and research opportunities to develop many of the strands of thought presented in this book. These ideas have also been developed through my teaching at the University of Nottingham, particularly in the modules 'Economic Geography' and 'Geographies of Money and Finance'. I would like to thank the students who have taken these modules and whose questions have helped me to refine my own research ideas. In Nottingham, I have been fortunate enough to work with the most supportive group of colleagues and I am also lucky enough to enjoy the support of a number of economic geographers more widely. In particular I would like to thank Andrew Leyshon, Adam Tickell, Louise Crewe, Shaun French, Adam Swain, Kean Fan Lim, Karen Lai, Jon Beaverstock, Jim Murphy, Al James, Andrew Jones, James Faulconbridge, Jane Pollard, Paul Langley, Brett Christophers, Lindsey Appleyard and Wendy Larner for their ongoing support. Robert Rojek and Matthew Oldfield at SAGE have been incredibly supportive of the project and extremely patient while I undertook the final revisions to the manuscript during maternity leave. Finally, I would like to thank my family and friends who continue to support me in raising three small children while working as an academic.

LIST OF ABBREVIATIONS

ABS	Alternative business structures
AIIB	Asian Infrastructure Investment Bank
BIS	Department for Business, Innovation and Skills
BVI	British Virgin Islands
CBRC	Chinese Banking Regulatory Commission
ESRC	Economic and Social Research Council
EU ETS	European Union Emissions Trading System
FDI	Foreign direct investment
FSA	Financial Services Authority
FSSC	Financial Services Skills Council
GATT	General Agreement on Tariffs and Trade
GFCI	Global Financial Centres Index
GPN	Global production network
HNWIs	High-net-worth individuals
HOLC	Home Owners' Loan Corporation
IBF	Islamic Banking and Finance
ICBC	Industrial and Commercial Bank of China
IFCs	International financial centres
ILS	Insurance-linked securities
IMF	International Monetary Fund
M&As	Mergers and Acquisitions
MBA	Master of Business Administration
OFCs	Offshore financial centres
OFT	Office of Fair Trading
PBOC	People's Bank of China
RMB	An abbreviation of renminbi, the official currency of the People's Republic of China
RMBS	Residential mortgage-backed securities
SIB	Securities and Investment Board
SMEs	Small and medium-sized enterprises
SROs	Self-regulatory organisations

1

INTRODUCTION

Chapter summary

- The end of finance as we knew it?
  - *From international financial relations to finance-led capitalism*
- Theoretical approaches to the changing nature of global finance
  - *Places, spaces and people in the making of financial markets*
- Global finance: looking forward

THE END OF FINANCE AS WE KNEW IT?

The financial crisis of 2007–2008 and the ensuing economic recession seemed, potentially, to signal the end of the international financial system as we knew it. The period in the run-up to the crisis represented a time of what appeared to be limitless growth within the global economy, and in the economies of Western Europe and North America in particular. Indeed, Mervyn King, the then Governor of the Bank of England, termed the 2000s the NICE decade (No Inflation, Constant Expansion decade). This period of growth had finance at its heart. As has become all too clear in the wake of the crisis, economic growth in the 2000s in much of Europe and North America was heavily reliant upon the provision of cheap credit to individuals, households and firms. The associated ease with which individuals could access mortgage finance in particular produced a buoyant housing market that in turn led to significant price inflation. For example, from 2000 until the height of housing market growth in July 2007, the UK typically saw annual house price inflation of 10 per cent (Land Registry, 2016). As a result, many households saw marked increases in their purchasing power, although those without wealth tied up in property faced growing economic uncertainty (Whitehead and Williams, 2011).

Within the international financial system itself, the 2000s were characterised by a period of significant change and innovation in terms of: the business models being utilised within financial firms and banks; the financial products being developed; and the labour markets associated with these (see Augar, 2009 for an overview of how these developments played out in London's financial district). Understanding the nature of these changes and their implications for both theoretical understandings of money and finance and the nature of the international financial system are the central concerns of this book.

FROM INTERNATIONAL FINANCIAL RELATIONS TO FINANCE-LED CAPITALISM

In order to understand the nature of the international financial system that was at the heart of the financial boom of the 2000s and the ensuing crisis, it is necessary to situate it within the longer recent history of international financial relations. Of particular significance in this respect is the Bretton Woods Agreement of 1944 and its collapse. This agreement, forged by economists and politicians from the USA and UK, sought to provide financial stability to the global economy and particularly the relationship between the USA and UK following the Second World War. There were two key elements to this agreement. First, a system of pegged exchange rates was facilitated through the US dollar being linked to the value of gold. This gave rise to the popular term the gold standard, in which the US dollar had a fixed exchange rate to gold and the rate of other currencies was, in turn, fixed to the US dollar. Second, this tightly controlled exchange rate system was supported by a range of multilateral organisations and agreements including the General Agreement on Tariffs and Trade (GATT), the International Bank for Reconstruction and Development, and the International Monetary Fund (IMF).

However, while the Bretton Woods Agreement was premised on the importance of maintaining a managed and predictable relationship between exchange rates in order to support economic growth, important internal contradictions were embedded within this agreement. In particular, there were tensions between individual state approaches to post-war development and the international nature of the agreement itself (Leyshon and Thrift, 1997). This became particularly apparent in terms of the creation of credit within the system as this increasingly shifted away from comparatively low-risk bank loans towards disintermediated, less easily 'managed' forms of credit provision. As a result, important new markets emerged that dealt with the growing circulation of offshore dollars: that is, beyond the borders of the USA. Here, development of the Euromarkets in London from the 1950s onwards is particularly significant as they signalled the ways in which the hegemony of the USA within the international financial system was increasingly being challenged. (For a fuller discussion of the rise of euro currency markets beyond the USA, see Burn, 1999; Schenk, 1998; and Chapter 2.) Consequently, by 1960, the value of US dollar reserves held domestically was less than the value of US dollar liabilities held beyond the boundaries of the USA.

As a result, the dollar's ability to act as the global reserve currency came under increasing pressure during the 1960s, a scenario that was further exacerbated by

---

BOX 1.1

KEY CHARACTERISTICS OF THE POST-BRETTON WOODS
INTERNATIONAL FINANCIAL SYSTEM

- Deep and dense networks between financial institutions, institutional investors, stock markets and new forms of financial intermediaries

  o Associated challenge to the hegemony of the US dollar

- Spatial paradox between the de-territorialisation of credit provision and the continued importance of a small number of international financial centres

- Crisis-prone nature of international financial system

- Changing multilateral governance arrangements

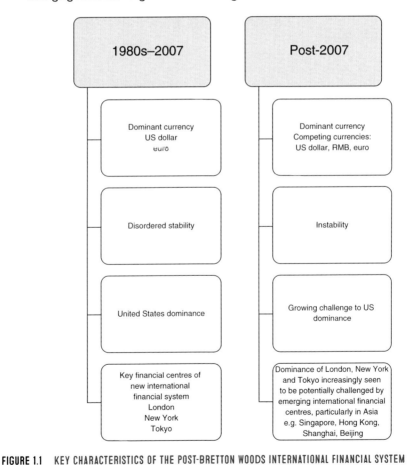

FIGURE 1.1 KEY CHARACTERISTICS OF THE POST-BRETTON WOODS INTERNATIONAL FINANCIAL SYSTEM

the increasing price of gold at this time. This ultimately led to the collapse of the Bretton Woods Agreement in 1973, and it is the international financial system that developed in the wake of this that forms the focus of this book (see Box 1.1). Four elements of the resulting contemporary international financial system are distinctive and underpin the arguments developed within the rest of this book.

First, the post-Bretton Woods period has been characterised by the development of a more intensely globally interconnected financial system. This system is increasingly structured around deep international networks that tie together a range of financial institutions, including global banking conglomerates, institutional investors (such as pension funds), stock markets, as well as the growth of new forms of important financial intermediaries and institutions including sovereign wealth funds, hedge funds and private equity firms. Within this system, the value of money is no longer tied to a commodity such as gold, as characterised the Bretton Woods era, and has moved to what are termed floating exchange rates. However, certainly until very recently, the US dollar and the euro have in effect acted as global reserve currencies, reflecting the economic and political power of the USA and Europe within the world economy.

In the post-financial-crisis era, important and significant questions have been raised about the ability of these currencies to maintain this role (discussed in more detail in Chapter 3). On the one hand, commentators have been quick to focus on the possibility of the Chinese currency, the renminbi, being able to challenge the US dollar and become the world's next global reserve currency. However, it is important to remember that there are still significant uncertainties surrounding the future trajectory of the development of the Chinese economy. These centre on: its ongoing restructuring away from a focus on manufacturing towards services; its relationship with other economies internationally, notably that of the USA; and the stability of the Chinese financial system in and of itself. The Shanghai stock market crisis in the summer of 2015 demonstrates these challenges clearly, when trading could only continue following the support of significant state intervention that was estimated to have cost more than US$800 billion of public and private funds (Reuters, 2015). Given the virtually unprecedented size of this intervention, it is uncertain if such activities are sustainable in the future.

Second, the post-Bretton Woods international financial system is characterised by a distinctive spatial paradox which involves the continued de-territorialisation of credit provision on the one hand, while also being increasingly anchored in a small number of cities, known as international financial centres, that act as the driving nodes within global finance, on the other. Chapter 2 examines the nature of these cities, particularly the dominance of New York and London and the relationship between these twin trends of de-territorialisation and concentration.

Third, the international financial system has also been characterised by its crisis-prone nature. For example, relatively quickly after the breakdown of the Bretton Woods Agreement, growing inflationary pressures precipitated the so-called 'less-developed country' debt crisis of the early 1980s in which a number of countries, including Brazil and Mexico, were unable to service their debts. Although this crisis initially started in the international financial system, and within international banks in particular, it is important to note that it had important implications for the everyday lives of people living in these countries in terms of its impacts on development trajectories. This represents an important early example within the international financial system of the ways in which finance is best understood not as an entirely separate realm from the rest of the economy. Indeed, although the international financial system has its own internal logic and illogic that need to be understood, it is important to appreciate how these shape socio-economic life more generally, a debate that is taken up in more detail in Chapters 5 and 7.

Fourth, there has been a growing appreciation of the ways in which international governance mechanisms have struggled to keep up with the internationalisation of the financial system. This has raised significant questions about the ability of multilateral and national institutions (such as the IMF and national financial policy makers) to act effectively in the wake of a number of financial crises. These include the Argentinian financial crisis of 1997, the dotcom bubble and burst in the early 2000s, and the Argentinian financial crisis of 2001, as well as the more recent crises of 2007–2008 and the ongoing euro crisis. An important focus for the rest of this book is understanding the interconnected nature of the international financial system and the ways in which particular financial practices, actors and places are tied together in periods of both growth and crisis, with significant implications for economic development at a range of scales from the household to regional and national economic development.

THEORETICAL APPROACHES TO THE CHANGING NATURE OF GLOBAL FINANCE

Given the size and scope of changes that have taken place within the financial system, it is unsurprising that there has been growing academic interest in money and finance across the social sciences. As a result, a range of different theoretical approaches has been developed. For example, critical social scientists across various disciplines have developed the concept of 'financialisation' to describe and explain the growing power of finance in shaping the global economy, often emphasising the deleterious consequences of such development for corporations and households as they become tied into ever more closer, yet precarious relationships with an increasingly unstable international financial system (see for example Froud et al., 2006; Langley, 2008). Meanwhile, other scholars have developed long-standing political economy work on money and finance through an international political economy approach to study what they label as the 'casino capitalism' nature of global finance (see Helleiner and Kirshner, 2014; Strange, 1986).

This book is grounded in a further approach to global finance which is usually labelled as 'cultural economy'. This interdisciplinary literature developed from the early 2000s onwards in a range of academic disciplines including sociology, economic geography, anthropology, politics and management. Reflecting the wider attention to questions of culture and society within studies of the economy at the time (for a wider discussion of cultural economy approaches, including those in money and finance, see Amin and Thrift, 2003), this body of research builds on a longer-standing commitment by social scientists to demonstrate how the economy is situated, or embedded, within social and cultural relations such that social, cultural and political worlds shape the nature of economic practices and decision making. For example, it is widely recognised that taken-for-granted assumptions about what counts as acceptable forms of financial practice vary between different cities as each has its own customs, social norms and regulations that serve to shape working behaviour (in the case of London, see Faulconbridge and Hall, 2014).

A cultural economy approach takes this interest in the social and cultural contexts of money and finance a stage further. Rather than locating the economy, or finance, within economic and social relations, cultural economy research argues that these different dimensions cannot be separated. Instead, the world of finance is understood as being constituted through the entanglement between economic, social and cultural relations (Hall, 2011). Based on the work of the French social theorist Michel Callon, particular emphasis is placed not only on the activities of humans in the construction of financial markets, but also on how humans interact with what are labelled 'non-human actors' as the world of finance is constantly in the process of being (re)produced (Caliskan and Callon, 2009; Callon, 2007). Examples of these non-human actors include financial formulae that are central to price setting and processes of valuation within markets (MacKenzie, 2003a, 2003b); the computer screens that traders use to receive information and make trades (Knorr Cetina and Bruegger, 2002); and the cables and supporting infrastructure that underpin the growing importance of high-frequency trading (MacKenzie, 2014). As such, a crucial and valuable insight from this literature is that financial markets do not come into the world preformed, but have to be actively made or assembled involving a range of different actors (for a fuller discussion of this approach to market making, see Berndt and Boeckler, 2009). Indeed, this approach has done much to move critical social science accounts of money and finance beyond macro-level description to a more detailed understanding of the ways in which financial markets are made and operate across a range of spatial scales.

However, more recently, and particularly in the wake of the 2007–2008 financial crisis, the cultural economy literature on money and finance has been increasingly criticised for potentially glamorising the world of high finance and not engaging critically with the politics of financial market making and their implications (Hall, 2011). In some ways, this neglect is not surprising because the main period in which this literature has been developed is precisely when international finance seemed to be characterised by significant innovations and continued growth in the 2000s in the run-up to the financial crisis. Moreover, the cultural economy literature developed mainly through a series of case studies that were located in the heartlands of global finance, notably the leading financial centres of New York,

London and Chicago. However, the outcomes of the financial crisis demand a more critical and politically attuned account of how markets are not only made, but also challenged, reproduced and transformed.

The account provided in this book argues that one important way in which such a critically informed cultural economy can be developed is through greater attention to the places, spaces and people involved in both making and experiencing the consequences of the continued development of the international financial system. This is important, since what seemed to start out as a sub-prime mortgage crisis focused on housing markets in the American south developed into a global credit crisis, widely dated back to the summer of 2007. For a period of time at least, this crisis stalled the expansion of financial services in a number of predominately Western European and North American countries and went on to trigger wider recessions in those countries that were heavily reliant on both cheap credit for households and firms for their economic growth.

The case of the UK demonstrates the severity of this downturn. In the early phases of the crisis, high street financial services providers that were household names, such as the building societies Northern Rock and Bradford and Bingley, were nationalised as they became unable to service their liabilities. This had particularly acute implications for the more peripheral regions of the UK beyond London and the south east where financial institutions such as Northern Rock were headquartered (see for example Dawley et al., 2014; Marshall, 2013). Meanwhile, confidence in the wholesale financial sector was severely damaged following the collapse of the investment bank Lehman Brothers in the USA in September 2008. Furthermore, in October 2008, the UK government announced a 'bailout' package for eight high street banks. Under this deal, these banks were collectively able to access £400 billion in additional capital, subject to changes in their business models which included signing agreements to limit their executive pay and bonuses; increasing their capital reserves; and issuing preference shares bought by the Treasury. Despite these early interventions, the UK's financial services sector continued to restrict credit and, in an effort to manage costs, both retail and wholesale financial institutions announced significant job cuts. In response, in January 2009, the government announced a package of further support for banks aimed at increasing credit liquidity, including powers for the Bank of England to make loans of up to £50 billion directly to businesses. These developments clearly raised a number of important questions concerning the sustainability and desirability of 'finance-driven capitalism' (Pike, 2006). Moreover, these events placed the relationship between ordinary households, firms and national economies, on the one hand, and the international financial system, on the other, in the political, media and academic spotlight. Indeed, people seemingly distant from the world of high finance, such as homeowners who could no longer access mortgage finance, and public sector workers facing redundancy as governments sought to fund bailouts for their banking system, found themselves experiencing the full effects of the crisis.

Moreover, the 2007–2008 financial crisis is often labelled, in popular, academic and media outlets, as a *global* financial crisis. However, the label of 'global' is in many ways erroneous. For example, although the crisis has undoubtedly had profound implications beyond its Anglo-American heartlands, for example through the ongoing eurozone crisis, it remains the case that the initial source of the crisis lay in the specific banking practices of investment banks in Wall Street and subsequently in London and other European banking centres (Tett, 2009). Meanwhile, the term global also hides the heterogeneous ways in which the crisis has affected different people in geographically variable ways. For example, research has revealed the disproportionate impact of the crisis on minority ethnic and racial groups in the USA in terms of the loss of their homes associated with the uncompetitive mortgage finance rates these groups were offered (Sidaway, 2008).

PLACES, SPACES AND PEOPLE IN THE MAKING OF FINANCIAL MARKETS

A focus on the places, spaces and people that are central to the making of financial markets provides a valuable way of developing more critical cultural economy understandings of global finance, particularly in the wake of the 2007–2008 financial crisis, because it draws attention to the power relations that are central to the making of financial markets. The first part of this book adopts such an approach to examine the changing nature of international financial centres (IFCs) as places within which the international financial system is produced. Chapter 2 argues that attending to the nature of work within IFCs demonstrates how cities such as London and New York have maintained their position at the heart of the international financial system, despite their role in causing the crisis. Then Chapter 3 examines the rise of important IFCs beyond these heartlands of global finance, notably in China in particular and Asia more broadly. In so doing, this chapter reveals the value of expanding the geographical focus of cultural economy research on finance beyond advanced economies in Europe and North America as other places become increasingly important in shaping the possible future direction of the international financial system.

The second part of the book focuses on the spaces and relational networks through which contemporary financial markets are made. First, in an effort to move beyond glamorising the world of high finance and treating it as a realm in and of itself, Chapter 4 examines work that has sought to break down a division between finance and the so-called 'real economy'. It does this by drawing on work on financialisation in particular. Subsequently, Chapter 5 builds on networks and relational understandings of finance to examine the changing and important role of offshore finance in shaping the post-crisis financial system. In so doing, this chapter builds on earlier chapters that seek to decentre cultural economy approaches to money and finance beyond Europe and North America while also revealing how it is increasingly difficult to make a neat separation between on- and offshore finance in the contemporary financial system. This insight has important implications for understanding where and how financial markets are made.

The third part of the book turns to the role of people in making and shaping financial markets. In Chapter 6, the focus is on the changing nature of financial elites both in terms of their role in making financial markets and through their consumption of financial services in the wealth management industry that has developed around them. Chapter 7 turns to the relationship between households and individuals who are seemingly rather far removed from the world of high finance. However, the analysis in this chapter examines how such individuals are increasingly tied into the international financial system through the range of financial products and services that they are increasingly expected to consume in order to secure their own financial and economic security in the face of significant cuts of public welfare schemes in a number of countries. In so doing, this chapter reveals how financial markets are made not only in IFCs, but also increasingly through the strategising and investment decisions made in everyday households. Chapter 8 reflects on the contribution cultural economic thinking has made to understandings of money and finance in the post-2007-8 financial crisis era as well as highlighting new forms of finance and their intsersection within wider economic development that will be important for cultural economy research to grapple with in the future.

GLOBAL FINANCE: LOOKING FORWARD

Clearly it is impossible to predict the future trajectory of global finance. Since at least the 1990s, the international financial system has been characterised by a series of crises interspersed with periods of significant growth and change. Indeed, the time since the 2007–2008 financial crisis has been no different. The crisis itself has developed into more entrenched financial difficulties, most notably through the euro crisis in which the ability of the euro to retain all of its constituent members has been brought into serious doubt. Meanwhile, a series of further geo-economic and geo-political transformations are likely to have a significant impact on finance. Within Europe, the vote to leave the EU by the UK following a referendum in June 2016 will shape the future of London's financial district in important ways as its ability to access the European Economic Area becomes a key issue in negotiations as the form the UK's exit from the EU (Brexit) is negotiated. Moreover, the possibility of China developing its currency into the next global reserve currency with the associated geo-political power shift that this would bring about has also been questioned because of significant concerns about the continued growth trajectory of the Chinese domestic economy. This has been demonstrated most clearly through the significant devaluation of the renminbi and ongoing concerns about the ability of the Chinese economy to maintain its growth rate as it restructures away from a reliance on the manufacturing sector to that of services.

However, at the same time, new financial spaces and actors are becoming increasingly important and seemingly escaping from the worst of the crisis. For example, long-standing financial centres such as London and New York have in many ways demonstrated considerable regenerative capacities as they continue to dominate the international financial system, not through the investment banking business models that dominated in the 2000s, but through the emergence of a range of new financial intermediaries, notably hedge funds (Folkman et al., 2007; Hall, 2009). Meanwhile new forms of financing associated with new financial technologies and platforms such as those developed with crowdfunding also pose significant challenges and opportunities to existing financial business models (Langley and Leyshon, 2016). The approach developed in this book provides some of the key theoretical and conceptual tools, grounded in a cultural economy approach, that will enable this ongoing development of the international financial system to be analysed and understood from a critical social science perspective. Moreover, such an approach should also always be open to the emergence of new places, spaces and people that develop and subsequently become some of the key actors in the continued (re)production of global finance.

KEY FURTHER READINGS

Hall, S. (2011) Geographies of money and finance I: cultural economy, politics and place. *Progress in Human Geography*, 35(2): 234–245.
This paper provides a critical overview of the development of cultural economy approaches to money and finance.

Leyshon, A. and Tickell, A. (1994) Money order? The discursive construction of Bretton Woods and the making and breaking of regulatory space. *Environment and Planning A*, 26(12): 1861–1890.
This paper provides more detail on the significance of the Bretton Woods Agreement to the shaping of the contemporary international financial system.

Pollard, J., McEwan, C., Laurie, N. and Stenning, A. (2009) Economic geography under postcolonial scrutiny. *Transactions of the Institute of British Geographers*, 34(2): 137–142.
This paper provides more detail on why it is important to decentre understandings of global finance beyond their focus on Europe and North America.

SECTION I

PLACING GLOBAL FINANCE: THE CHANGING ROLE OF INTERNATIONAL FINANCIAL CENTRES

2

INTERNATIONAL FINANCIAL CENTRES AND THE REPRODUCTION OF GLOBAL FINANCE

Chapter summary

- The changing structure of global finance

    o   *Understanding the changing nature of global finance*

- The spatial paradoxes of global finance

- Placing international financial centres within the International financial system

    o   *The post-war international financial system and the role of IFCs*

    o   *Understanding the reproduction of IFCs*

- The changing nature of London as an international financial centre

    o   *From merchant to investment banking in London's financial district*

    o   *The rise of the investment banking business model in London's IFC*

    o   *From financialised growth to post-crisis transformation*

- Conclusions

THE CHANGING STRUCTURE OF GLOBAL FINANCE

The key functions, and associated structure, of the international financial system have changed markedly over time. Much of this transformation is closely related to the emergence of different functions for money and finance. Indeed, it is surprisingly difficult to answer the seemingly straightforward question 'What is money?' How this question is approached and answered and the forms that money and finance take have profound implications for the nature of global finance.

From a political economy perspective, money and its associated financial circuits are essential in facilitating the circuits of production and exchange that underpin the wider economy. In these accounts money acts as

> a medium of exchange and as a measure of value. ... Therefore, money lubricates the circuit of productive capital, providing both free exchange between a wide range of commodities and a universally recognisable medium. However, money is much more than just a signatory to an exchange of commodities. To be a medium of exchange money must also be a measure of value, otherwise the process of exchange would not be possible. (Leyshon and Thrift, 1997: 44)

One important way in which this function of money and finance has been performed, historically at least, is through intermediation, which has been at the heart of the function of banking:

> The credit system, through the intermediation of financial institutions, helps mobilise money as capital through the centralisation of previously individualised stores of money, which on their own would be insufficient to kick the circuit of productive capital to life.

However, from the 1970s onwards, banks have faced growing competition from non-bank financial intermediaries and, as a result, the financial system has become increasingly disintermediated in nature. This means that credit, particularly in the forms of bonds and securitised finance, is increasingly accessed directly from investors rather than through banks. As a result, investors, including pension funds and insurance companies, have become increasingly important actors within global finance. As Figure 2.1 demonstrates, this change has been accompanied by significant developments in the form that banking takes and its relationship to the creation of credit within the international financial system more generally.

Indeed, such is the importance of new forms of finance and credit provision that the nature of international finance can increasingly be understood through a focus on the securities industry building on Stages 6 and 7 of Figure 2.1. As Figure 2.2 shows, although investment banks are critical to this subsector of the international financial system, they operate alongside a number of other agents including brokers, stock exchanges, pension funds, mutual funds and investment advisors.

UNDERSTANDING THE CHANGING NATURE OF GLOBAL FINANCE

There are four main characteristics of the resulting contemporary international financial system:

The stages of banking development	Banks and space	Credit and space
Stage 1: Pure financial intermediation		
Banks lend out savings. Payment in commodity money. No bank multiplier. Saving precedes investment.	Serving local communities. Wealth-based, providing foundation for future financial centres.	Intermediation only.
Stage 2: Bank deposits used as money		
Convenient to use paper money as means of payment. Reduced drain on bank reserves. Multiplier process possible. Bank credit creation with fractional reserves. Investment can now precede saving.	Market dependent on extent of confidence held in banker.	Credit creation focused on local community because total credit constrained by redeposit ratio.
Stage 3: Inter-bank lending		
Credit creation still constrained by reserves. Risk of reserves loss offset by development of inter-bank lending. Multiplier process works more quickly. Multiplier larger because banks can hold lower reserves.	Banking system develops at national level.	Redeposit constraint relaxed somewhat, so can lend wider afield.
Stage 4: Lender-of-last-resort facility		
Central bank perceives need to promote confidence in banking system. Lender-of-last-resort facility provided if inter-bank lending inadequate. Reserves now respond to demand. Credit creation freed from reserves constraint.	Central bank oversees national system, but limited power to constrain credit.	Banks freer to respond to credit demand as reserves constraint not binding and they can determine volume and distribution of credit within national economy.
Stage 5: Liability management		
Competition from non-bank financial intermediaries drives struggle for market share. Banks actively supply credit and seek deposits. Credit expansion diverges from real economic activity.	Banks compete at national level with non-bank financial institutions.	Credit creation determined by struggle over market share and opportunities in speculative markets. Total credit uncontrolled.
Stage 6: Securitisation		
Capital adequacy ratios introduced to curtail credit. Banks have an increasing proportion of bad loans because of over-lending in Stage 5. Securitisation of bank assets. Increase in off-balance-sheet activity. Drive to liquidity.	Deregulation opens up international competition, eventually causing concentration in financial centres.	Shift to liquidity by emphasis being put on services rather than credit; credit decisions concentrated in financial centres; total credit determined by availability of capital, i.e. by central capital markets.
?	?	?
Stage 7: Response to 2008 crisis		
Potential for redrawing of boundaries between different banking functions.	Possible re-regulation at national and/or international scales.	Possible re-focus on lending to domestic borrowers.

FIGURE 2.1 THE SEQUENCE OF DEVELOPMENT OF THE BANKING SYSTEM

Source: P. Dicken, *Global Shift* (Sage: 7th edition, 2015), based in part on Dow (1999, Tables 1 and 2)

an intensified level of competition between financial agents; increasingly sophisticated means of issuing and using debt; financial innovation linked to the management and exploitation of risk; and the importance of volatility as a means of amplifying both profits and losses. (Leyshon and Thrift, 1997: 201)

Understanding the development of this form of global finance requires examining the changing governance and regulatory frameworks surrounding international finance from the middle of the twentieth century onwards. Central in this respect is the Bretton Woods Agreement, as we briefly saw in Chapter 1. This agreement represented the construction of an 'international regulated space' (Leyshon and Thrift, 1997: 71) that shaped the international financial system from its creation in 1944 until the late 1960s (although fixed exchange rates ended in the 1950s). However, although the period governed by the Bretton Woods Agreement is often associated with a period of comparative stability within international financial markets, this system was inherently contradictory from the start, not least in terms of the role of the USA as both the guarantor for the system and a significant geo-economic power within the system with its own geo-economic interests (Leyshon and Thrift, 1997). These tensions were most marked in terms of the circulation of US dollars in the global economy. US dollars began to circulate in growing volumes within the global economy, not least as a result of the Marshall Plan. Through this plan, the USA sought to provide financial and trade support to states in Western Europe in order to support the activities of US manufacturing firms while simultaneously seeking to limit the growth of communism in Eastern Europe. At the same time, several states were cautious about returning dollars to the USA for fear that these financial assets would be the source of interest for the US regulatory authorities. As a result, a series of money and credit markets developed that escaped both national and international regulation in the form of euro currency markets. These markets involved both states and multinational firms issuing debt in offshore US dollars and, importantly for the arguments in this chapter, London played a central role in their development through hosting such markets (Burn, 1999; Schenk, 1998).

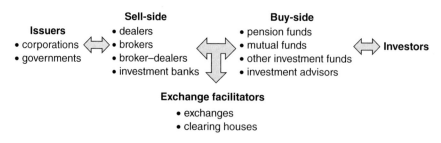

FIGURE 2.2   THE BASIC STRUCTURE OF THE SECURITIES INDUSTRY

Source: Wójcik (2012)

These euro currency markets placed increased pressures on the Bretton Woods regulatory arrangements. In particular, while dollars circulating beyond the USA in part facilitated economic recovery in a number of nation states, it also led to a degree of economic competition between states that did not sit easily with the international collaboration that underpinned the Bretton Woods Agreement. The growth of this finance capital beyond US boundaries also led to inflationary pressures within domestic, national economies, and the amount of finance capital circulating began to outstrip the funds available to the IMF and the World Bank, thereby limiting the geo-economic and geo-political power of these institutions.

Collectively, these pressures led to the collapse of the Bretton Woods regulatory order in 1971 when the USA abandoned the gold standard of the dollar (ending the ability to convert dollars into gold) which, in 1973, led to the collapse of the fixed exchange system. It was the end of this regulatory order that led to the development of a much enlarged international financial system in which forms of credit money have become increasingly important that are international and de-territorialised in their regulatory control. This process began in the 1950s with the growing importance of institutional investors such as pension funds and insurance companies, but accelerated from the late 1970s onwards after the collapse of the Bretton Woods Agreement. Following the growth of the euro currency markets, financial institutions increased their issuance of credit. These developments gave way to a distinctive geography, or spatial footprint, of global finance with states becoming less able to control and manage the international financial system as it increasingly operated across and beyond national boundaries. However, at the same time, small international financial centres within cities became increasingly important spaces in the production of this international financial system.

THE SPATIAL PARADOXES OF GLOBAL FINANCE

What is commonly termed global finance, or the new international financial system following the collapse of the Bretton Woods Agreement, contains two important spatial paradoxes. First, despite being termed global finance, the international financial system is coordinated through a small number of financial districts within large cities. The most important and powerful of these financial districts, namely the international financial centres (IFCs), are those found in New York and London (GFCI, 2014). The financial districts within these two IFCs have, since at least the early twentieth century, dominated and shaped global flows of finance, containing the most significant clusters of financial and related legal firm headquarters accompanied by the necessary infrastructure to support these financial activities. This includes a regulatory regime that supports the financial services sector, suitable office accommodation and financial institutions such as stock markets and clearing banks (Wójcik, 2007; 2009). This spatial form counters claims that we are witnessing the 'end of geography' (O'Brien, 1991). This thesis claims that the importance of location in shaping financial services activity is diminishing because of technological innovation and deregulation that would, so the argument goes, allow financial firms to be more 'footloose' in their location strategies as money becomes increasingly de-territorialised and as communication and information technology facilitated the increasing provision of financial services remotely.

Indeed, the financial districts of London and New York have shown considerable ability, historically at least, in maintaining their dominance, despite several instances during which it appeared to be challenged. For example, following the launch of the euro, it was at first thought that Frankfurt might rise to prominence above London within Europe (Faulconbridge, 2004). Meanwhile, in the immediate aftermath of the 2007–2008 financial crisis, speculation grew that the Middle East might provide the next leading IFC, particularly in the form of Dubai as it transformed itself from an industrial city state based around petroleum to an advanced service sector, post-industrial economy (Pacione, 2005). However, Dubai itself became one of the major casualties of the financial crisis and its financial services cluster is now particularly focused on the provision of Islamic finance (see Chapter 3). This dynamism in terms of potential new challenger financial centres to London and New York has continued, although the focus has increasingly turned to Asia, notably Singapore and Hong Kong, and to a lesser extent Beijing and Shanghai, which are increasing their influence within the international financial system (GFCI, 2014; Lai, 2012). Meanwhile, following the financial crisis, in addition to the continued importance of both established and emerging IFCs, offshore financial spaces have become an increasingly important component of global finance, often associated with close relationships with their onshore counterparts (see Chapter 5).

The second spatial paradox within global finance lies within the nature of IFCs themselves. In this respect, they are typically identified by their city name, such as London and New York. However, their financial services cluster and associated financial power are typically concentrated in a very small part of the city. These small enclaves are, therefore, disproportionally powerful when compared with their material urban footprint. For example, New York's financial district, Wall Street, is focused on Midtown Manhattan with an increasing number of back office functions being located in New Jersey. London's financial district has historically been called the City – denoting a square mile area centred on the Bank of England to the east of the centre of London (hence its colloquial name, the Square Mile). However, London's financial district now extends eastwards to include Canary Wharf, west into Mayfair where a number of hedge funds, asset managers and private wealth managers are located, and north to Silicon Roundabout around Old Street Underground Station where there is a growing cluster of financial technology companies. Furthermore, emerging financial centres are deliberately developing their own financial clusters within city boundaries, such as the Dubai International Financial Centre (Engelen and Glasmacher, 2013).

In addition to academic research seeking to explain the continued importance of a relatively small number of different forms of financial centres, these spatial paradoxes have also given rise to a significant consultancy industry that seeks to rank financial districts. The most well-known ranking is the GFCI (Global Financial

TABLE 2.1 TOP 10 GLOBAL FINANCIAL CENTRES INDEX (GFCI) RANKINGS, 2007 AND 2014

Financial centre	2014 ranking	2007 ranking	Change in position
New York	1	2	+1
London	2	1	−1
Hong Kong	3	3	−
Singapore	4	4	−
San Francisco	5	13	+8
Tokyo	6	9	+3
Zurich	7	5	−2
Seoul	8	43	+35
Boston, MA	9	14	+5
Washington, DC	10	20	+10

Source: GFCI (2007; 2014)

Centres Index) published annually since 2007 by the consultancy firm Z/Yen using a number of criteria, including business environment (which includes elements such as regulation), human capital (which focuses on the depth of highly skilled labour markets in any given centre) and the reputation of the centre among financiers (see Table 2.1). These rankings are important to the political and urban authorities responsible for promoting their respective financial centres. Indeed, the perceived economic and political importance of hosting a leading IFC is reflected in an increasingly diverse range of tactics used by such bodies to enhance the reputation of their particular centre, including the use of imagery to market financial centres alongside dedicated websites (Engelen and Glasmacher, 2013).

PLACING INTERNATIONAL FINANCIAL CENTRES WITHIN THE INTERNATIONAL FINANCIAL SYSTEM

THE POST-WAR INTERNATIONAL FINANCIAL SYSTEM AND THE ROLE OF IFCs

The existence of IFCs is not a new phenomenon in the international financial system. For example, London's financial cluster can be dated back to the 1700s and increased as the City developed as a key financial centre in support of the British Empire, offering financial services to support trade (McRae and Cairncross, 1985). That said, in academic, policy and practitioner communities the term tends to get used frequently but is not commonly defined. An IFC can be understood as a distinctive district within a city that has a high degree of concentration of financial and related professional services (such as corporate law firms). The precise composition of IFCs varies, although they typically include a range of financial institutions and regulators, banks (including commercial, wholesale and private banks), institutional investors including pension funds, a stock exchange and traders. In order to understand the enduring significance of IFCs, it is necessary to position their development within the wider trajectory of the development of the contemporary international financial system.

UNDERSTANDING THE REPRODUCTION OF IFCs

Social science work on the international financial system, and the role of IFCs within this, has built on the seminal work of David Harvey (1982) in which he focused on the changing geo-politics that shape the international financial system and, in particular, how place-specific regulatory environments and their associated working cultures produce both on- and offshore financial centres (offshore financial centres are considered in more detail in Chapter 5). From this starting point, two complementary approaches have developed. First, research has examined the benefits of agglomeration for financial firms and agents that gives rise to, and sustains, financial clusters within IFCs (Cook et al., 2007). This research builds on the identification of different types of knowledge that are central to the (re)production and use of financial products (Clark and O'Connor, 1997). In particular, many of the financial products that make up the international financial system, such as the collateralised debt obligations that underpin the processes of securitisation that were central to the 2007–2008 financial crisis, are opaque in nature. This means that considerable knowledge asymmetries develop between the producers and consumers of financial products so that consumers frequently know more than financial services providers about the nature and demands of the financial products being developed. As a result, financial firms co-locate within IFCs in order to develop financial innovations and products that involve drawing on the networks that cut across financial firms and their corporate clients, as well as other forms of expertise, particularly those provided by corporate lawyers. These activities also include other sources of information, notably informal knowledge about the taken-for-granted working cultures and practices of the clients and the financial cluster itself in order that products can be tailored to highly specific client requirements. As a result, financial centres produce such a 'buzz' that dense interpersonal and interfirm relations play a central role in service delivery as well as innovation, because financiers use these networks to understand better the demands of their clients and the developments being made by their competitor firms. In this way, these relations are quite unusual as they comprise relations of both collaboration and competition.

In addition to this focus on intra-cluster dynamics within IFCs, the second area of research on financial clusters focuses on inter-cluster relationships and the contribution of these relations in maintaining the dominance of a small number of IFCs. This approach builds on wider work on the networked nature of the contemporary economy that develops further the relations of both competition and collaboration between IFCs. As Wójcik (2013: 2) summarises, 'from this perspective, international financial centres are viewed as a spatially distributed network of money and power, where the global and local processes intermesh and run into each other in a variety of ways'. This work has been developed most fully through what is known as the NY–LON (New York–London) connection (Beaverstock, 2005; Wójcik, 2013). Nevertheless, a series of other relations have been identified as being important, such as the challenge posed to London's dominance as the leading European IFC by Frankfurt in the wake of the creation of the eurozone (Faulconbridge, 2004). More recently this approach has been applied to rapidly growing financial centres, particularly in Asia, including Singapore, Hong Kong, Beijing and Shanghai (Lai, 2012). A number of different measures have been used to understand these connections, including the global office networks of leading financial institutions and law firms, the geographies of stock markets that in many ways anchor IFCs, and the flows of highly skilled individuals through migration and expatriation that support the development of specialist labour markets in IFCs (Beaverstock, 2004).

This work explains why IFCs exist, documents the emergence of important new powerful centres and demonstrates the ways in which these centres are underpinned by dense relations both within and between centres. However, less attention has been paid to the dynamic nature of IFCs and the specificity of different IFCs. One valuable way of addressing this is to focus on the role of highly skilled individuals working in financial centres.

Building on this work, this chapter draws on the insights from a cultural economy approach to money and finance outlined in Chapter 1 to examine how the relationship between regulatory change and working practices provides a valuable way of understanding the *distinctiveness* of particular financial centres in which certain forms of financial activity are deemed legitimate and desirable (Dixon, 2014). This focus is important because the distinctive working cultures of leading IFCs in the 2000s have been labelled as important factors in both creating the financial crisis and transmitting it beyond its US heartland (Wainwright, 2009). Based on these observations, the analysis below focuses on the case of London's international financial district in order to demonstrate the importance of understanding the distinct cultures associated with different financial centres and the ways in which these contribute to a continually variegated international financial system (see Zald and Lounsbury, 2010). In so doing, a focus on how particular forms of finance and their associated working cultures develop over time in specific financial centres in conjunction with regulatory changes responds to calls that understandings of money and finance need to develop more nuanced understandings of the 'globalisation of money' that 'reconceptualise monetary space [to] map its different layers and dimensions, its various constituent subspaces, and the myriad interconnections among them' (Dodd, 2014: 221).

THE CHANGING NATURE OF LONDON AS AN INTERNATIONAL FINANCIAL CENTRE

Despite the different approaches to understanding why IFCs are important, a common factor in this literature is an appreciation of the importance of highly skilled labour to securing the vitality and competitiveness of IFCs (Hall, 2009). For example, in the wake of the financial crisis, employment in financial services including insurance in the City of London (excluding Canary Wharf) increased from 136,700 in 2009 to 159,300 in 2012 before declining slightly in 2013 to 147,600 (City of London, 2015). Indeed, the importance of highly skilled work is reflected in the rhetoric that surrounds these labour markets, with statements from both trade organisations and employing firms underlining the centrality of highly skilled workers to the competitiveness of individual organisations and the City of London more generally.

However, while these figures demonstrate the recovery of financial services following the financial crisis, behind the numbers lies an important story about how the nature of work itself has changed within financial services, with significant implications for revealing the changing nature of the international financial system. The case of London provides a particularly useful lens through which to examine these changes, demonstrating how a focus on the nature of work within financial centres is a valuable way of understanding how IFCs are reproduced. In so doing, a practice-orientated approach is valuable because it focuses on how certain forms of action and associated cultures become legitimised and valued in particular times at particular places (for a summary of this approach, see Faulconbridge and Hall, 2014; Gherardi, 2009; Jones and Murphy, 2010; Shove, 2003; Wenger, 1998). Two key moments of transition within London's financial district are the focus of the case study analysis below: first, the run-up to and fallout from the deregulatory changes of the mid-1980s, collectively known as Big Bang; and second, the financialised boom of the 2000s and ensuing fallout from the financial crisis.

FROM MERCHANT TO INVESTMENT BANKING IN LONDON'S FINANCIAL DISTRICT

Dating back to at least the post-war period, London's financial labour markets have been characterised as being based around a form of 'gentlemanly capitalism' (Augar, 2001). At one level, this term stems from the highly gendered nature of financial labour markets, something that persists to the present day (Jones, 1998; McDowell, 1997). However, it also speaks to the distinctive recruitment practices within financial labour markets in London's financial district up until at least the significant deregulatory changes of 1987, collectively known as Big Bang (discussed in more detail below). Until this point, it is argued that recruitment into finance was based upon a shared social and education background between the recruiter and the new hire at a small number of elite, fee-paying (public) schools and Oxford and Cambridge Universities (Oxbridge). However, the importance of 'gentlemanly capitalism' extended beyond recruitment, and these 'old boys' networks' were important in facilitating the development of trust-based relationships between financiers (Cain and Hopkins, 1987; Michie, 1992). As Thrift (1994: 342) notes, this 'narrative of the gentleman' was 'based on values of honour, integrity, courtesy and so on, and manifested in ideas of how to act, ways to talk [and] suitable clothing' (see also Tickell, 1996).

At the time, this version of 'gentlemanly capitalism' was particularly important because the City was dominated by merchant banking in terms of the business models that were influential then. Merchant banks in London were typically English or European-owned firms that focused on a relationship model of banking in which the corporate client would typically use one bank for all its banking activities, including loans, current account, deposits and payments. Indeed, the ability to purvey trustworthiness within this world of 'measured calm' was central both in the formation of interpersonal networks within financial services at this time and to the development of trust-based relationships vital for financial-services product development in particular (Michie, 1992). For example, it has been argued that 'gentlemanly capitalism' underpinned London's historically light touch approach to regulation in which the Bank of England was based within close proximity of the banks it was regulating such that the Bank could use this proximity to fulfil its regulatory requirements based on a shared understanding between financiers and the Bank that a 'gentleman's word was his bond' (see Pryke, 1991). As Moran writes:

> British banking regulation contrasted markedly with the regulatory systems of other economically advanced nations. It worked by informal agreements and understandings, emphasised flexibility in rule-making and operated almost totally without legal sanctions. (1991: 56)

However, it is important to note that although the discourse of 'gentlemanly capitalism' is typically used to characterise the nature of the City of London up until the regulatory changes of the mid-1980s, things began to change throughout the 1970s. For example, the Parliamentary Select Committee on nationalised industries started to show an increasing interest in the Bank of England from 1968 onwards, particularly given its position as a stronghold of traditional 'gentlemanly capitalism' (Spiegelberg, 1973). Despite being nationalised in 1945, the Bank retained the majority of the traits of a private company. For example, it did not charge the government (its customer) the true cost of providing its services as was standard practice among other nationalised industries. Moreover, there was nothing in the Bank's charter at the time of nationalisation suggesting that it should disclose its financial accounts or the salaries of full-time directors. The directors themselves also represented a particular cadre of finance professionals, with all but two previously working as merchant bankers – a situation that did not change until 1983 (Burn, 1999). The select committee published a report on the Bank of England in May 1970 in which it portrayed the Bank as

> an arcane assortment of machinery which not so much defined, as operated outside, the normal laws of commercial activity. (Spiegelberg, 1973: 148)

The UK government demonstrated its support for the main principles of this report in a White Paper published in March 1971, in which it made clear its expectations that the Bank would make charges to cover the full cost of its services to the government. The Treasury was also to be informed of the Bank's programme of capital expenditure. In return, however, the Bank's regulatory power remained virtually untouched (Clarke, 2001; Collins, 1991). As a result, the Bank began to abandon its 'traditional, informal and unsystematic system of supervision for a more detailed and elaborate set of rules administered by a professional staff of regulators backed by legal powers' (Moran, 1991: 67). These changes can be classified as increased codification (the rise of formal and more complicated rules), increased institutionalisation (the growth of regulatory bodies) and increased juridification (the placing of rules on the Statute book and hence giving them legal powers) (Moran, 1991).

Indeed, it was the 1970s that saw the foundation of the changes that brought about Big Bang as calls increased for a more independent and professional approach to regulation within the City and from the Bank in particular. The seeds of Big Bang were laid in the Fair Trading Act of 1973, which established the Office of Fair Trading (OFT), to advocate an ideology of free-market competition (Moran, 1991; Roberts and Kynaston, 2001). The jurisdiction of the OFT was increased to include service industries and, therefore, the London Stock Exchange, in 1976. The London Stock Exchange unsuccessfully lobbied for an exemption. In July 1983, an agreement between the Trade and Industry Secretary Cecil Parkinson and the Chairman of the Stock Exchange, Sir Nicholas Goodison, allowed the London Stock Exchange to remain outside the jurisdiction of the OFT on the condition that it amended the rules that the OFT had objected to, namely the abolition of fixed commission rates by December 1986, thereby changing the nature of competitive practice within the Stock Exchange (Vogel, 1996). Two further rules were abolished on 27 October 1986, namely the 'single capacity' system that enforced the separation between brokers (agents for buyers and sellers of stock) and jobbers (dealers as principals), and the prohibition on outsiders holding more than a minority stake in member firms, allowing banks and foreign financial institutions to purchase them outright for the first time. The domestic securities industry subsequently transformed from a small, independent and UK-owned outfit to one made up of subsidiaries from multinational conglomerates (Vogel, 1996).

The Goodison–Parkinson agreement, as the change above become known, demanded a new regulatory framework. This was provided by the Financial Services Act (1986), which changed the institutional setting of financial regulation in the UK from a dispersed system of meso-corporatism loosely coordinated by the Bank to a system of codification, institutionalisation and juridification (Moran, 1991). However, in many ways, the Act represented an acceleration and intensification of changes to the banking establishment within the City that had started with the Bank's nationalisation in 1946 as it became apparent that the Bank's ad hoc, trust-based regulatory system was not suitable to the post-war banking climate. The contents of the reforms were a response to and mirrored those that had already taken place in the USA – a further example of how the changes were driven by a desire to maintain London's competitiveness vis-à-vis New York.

The Act was passed on 7 November 1986, creating a new, private regulatory agency to which statutory powers were delegated, the Securities and Investment Board (SIB), which, in turn, authorised and supervised five self-regulatory organisations (SROs). Financial firms acquired a licence to operate by being accepted as a member of the appropriate SRO. The importance of the Act should not be understated, as noted by Vogel (1996: 93):

> The FSA may have revolutionized life in the City even more than Big Bang, for in matters of regulation it replaced the informal with the formal, the flexible with the rigid, and the personal with the legalistic.

These developments demonstrate that the regulatory changes collectively known as Big Bang echo more recent scholarship on processes of neoliberalisation in which it is seen as both the simultaneous rolling back of some state regulations and the rolling out of new forms of regulation (Peck and Tickell, 2002). Indeed, Big Bang can be conceived of as including both deregulation and re-regulation rather than a narrower account of diminishing state power in the face of evermore omnipresent global markets:

> In the space of two weeks in the autumn of 1986, London experienced the boldest of both: the abolition of restrictive practices by the Stock Exchange *and* the inauguration of a new, more extensive and intrusive system of regulation. (Vogel, 1996: 93)

At first, the changes wrought by Big Bang seemed to have strengthened the UK-owned merchant and now investment banks. However, the crash of October 1987 forced a further change in the ownership and business practices of these UK institutions. The US banks increased their London presence from the late 1980s onwards. For example, between 1986 and 1989, Merrill Lynch increased the number of its London-based staff from 760 to 1,600 while, over the same period, Goldman Sachs increased the number of its employees in London from 520 to 744 (Roberts and Kynaston, 2001). The US investment banks were trying to position themselves to take full advantage of a perceived growth in investment banking activity in the face of European economic integration.

Structural changes within the banks also affected their social composition (Augar, 2001; Thrift, 1994):

> In a broader sense, the Big Bang symbolized a cultural shift that had begun long before that day in 1986 and would continue long after. The gentleman's luncheon was replaced by the power breakfast, civilized rivalry was replaced by cutthroat competition and discrete self-regulation was replaced by a nightmare from America: the proliferation of regulatory bodies, the endless creation of rules, and an invasion of lawyers. (Vogel, 1996: 108)

However, the supposed death of gentlemanly capitalists (Augar, 2001; Thrift, 1994), in favour or a more egalitarian and meritocratic system, does not refer to the same gentlemen who were at the helm of the merchant banking industry at the turn of the twentieth century, as is often assumed to be the case (Michie, 1992). It is actually a shorter-term change between the leading bankers after the Second World War and those running the industry in the wake of Big Bang. For instance, the role played by the Midland Bank in the rise of the Eurodollar markets demonstrates that the market-leading banks after the war were not limited to the family merchant banking houses that the industry had been built around in the nineteenth century.

THE RISE OF THE INVESTMENT BANKING BUSINESS MODEL IN LONDON'S IFC

Big Bang also heralded a change in industry nomenclature from merchant to investment banking, reflecting fundamental changes in the nature and organisation of the business. Prior to the widespread regulatory changes of the early 1980s in London and New York, they referred to different styles of banking, each with its own history and geography. Merchant banking was used in reference to UK- or European-owned firms that had become established brands in London, dating back to the nineteenth century, while investment banking was used in the USA. Merchant banking was a predominantly *relationship*- and *trust*-based industry where business was built on long-term client–advisor relationships (Roberts and Kynaston, 2001). Once a working relationship had been established between a client and its bank, it was mutually understood that future financial services would be purchased from that bank at the expense of competitors. Merchant banks tended to undertake client-based, fee-paying, largely advisory activities that were characterised as comparatively low-risk business lines demanding relatively low levels of capital. Unlike their European counterparts, the UK merchant banks did not establish their own commercial banks.

Conversely, investment banking in the USA has historically been *transaction* and *cost* based. In this model, banks bid aggressively for each client mandate as a one-off piece of business, enabling potential clients to select a different investment bank whenever they want to undertake a financial transaction. As a result, investment banks learnt how to 'pitch' business ideas to potential clients in an effort to win the contract for that piece of business at the expense of their rivals. Therefore, US investment banks tended to bid aggressively for each business mandate as a one-off piece of business, not forming part of an ongoing client–advisor relationship. As a business model, the US approach was seen as riskier and more capital intensive, but it was pro-cyclical: during periods of financial expansion, business was highly profitable, but periods of contraction saw aggressive pricing and significant financial losses.

Until the mid-1980s, US investment banks had a marginal presence in London. This changed following regulatory developments in the early 1980s. Restrictions on the ownership of London Stock Exchange firms were relaxed under Big Bang in 1986, allowing banks to purchase them for the first time (Roberts and Kynaston, 2001). Indeed, between 1983 and 1986, the majority of leading securities firms (with the exception of Cazenove and Smith Brothers) were bought by foreign parties, including 14 by US investment banks (see Figure 2.3) (Roberts and Kynaston, 2001). Using their newly increased market share, US and, later, European investment securities firms were companies whose operations specialised in the issuing and trading of international bonds and equities rather than advisory work on mergers and acquisitions for corporate clients (Clarke, 2001). These investment banks squeezed UK merchant banks' market share on two fronts. First, the growing US banking presence in London led to increased competition between the banks for staff, driving up salaries. Second, as competition for business increased, the fees charged by banks were driven down. US banks could use their profits from Wall Street, where fee levels were on average higher than in London, to bid aggressively for both staff and business. As a consequence, from the mid-1980s onwards, almost all UK merchant banks were purchased by overseas competitors.

UK merchant banks responded to the changes wrought by Big Bang in different ways. Former UK merchant banks which chose to pursue an integrated, investment banking approach included Morgan Grenfall, Barings, Kleinwort, Warburg and Hambros. They were joined in the integrated model by UK clearing banks including Barclays, NatWest and Midland Bank. However, the established business pattern was continued by the merchant banks Schroders, Lazard and Fleming and by the stockbroker Cazenove (Kynaston, 2002; Roberts and Kynaston, 2001).

These upheavals brought about changes in both the types of masculinity performed in financial services workplaces in the City of London and the ways in which financiers were recruited. Beginning with recruitment, the diversification of

UK firm	Purchaser	Year	Price (£ million)
Morgan Grenfall	Deutsche Bank	1989	950
Barings	ING	1995	£1 plus liabilities*
Warburg	Swiss Bank Corporation	1995	860
Kleinwort Benson	Dresdner Bank	1995	1,000
Smith New Court	Merrill Lynch	1995	526
BZW (Barclays-part)	CSFB	1997	100
NatWest markets (part)	Bankers Trust/Deutsche Bank	1997	129
Hambros	Société Générale/Investec	1997	738
Mercury Asset Management	Merrill Lynch	1997	3,100
Schroders (part)	Citigroup	2000	1,350
Fleming	Chase Manhattan	2000	4,800

*not million

FIGURE 2.3 SALE OF UK FINANCIAL FIRMS, 1989-2000

Source: Roberts and Kynaston (2001:96)

ownership in financial firms and the expansion in the number of institutions meant that the labour market demands in terms of numbers could no longer be met through the established recruitment channels that restricted the search for candidates to a small number of public schools and Oxbridge (Leyshon and Thrift, 1997). As a result, there was a diversification, albeit limited in nature, of increasing recruitment from a wider range of universities, focusing primarily on the elite Russell Group of universities in the UK (Hall and Appleyard, 2009; 2011; Jones, 1998). Moreover, while the dominant form of masculinity associated with merchant banking was that of 'gentlemanly capitalism', by the 1990s, the more transactional rather than relationship-based business model of investment banking had given rise to the performance of multiple masculinities within London's financial district (McDowell, 1997). In particular, the rapid growth of trading as a set of financial activities meant that a younger, more outwardly aggressive, macho masculinity was increasingly found in the City.

FROM FINANCIALISED GROWTH TO POST-CRISIS TRANSFORMATION

A focus on the labour markets of London (and other IFCs) and their response to regulatory change is not only instructive in demonstrating this earlier phase of transformation in financial business models, but also very powerful in revealing the transformation in wholesale finance within IFCs in the run-up to and following the financial crisis of 2007-2008. Prior to this crisis, the US investment banking model led the development of leading financial centres, notably New York and London. For example, in 2006, immediately prior to the financial crisis, figures suggest that around 354,000 people were employed in wholesale financial services in the UK (FSSC, 2007). However, the financial crisis both temporarily stalled the growth of this 'finance-led capitalism' (Pike, 2006) and led to a transformation in the institutions and organisations operating within IFCs such as London. In particular, the investment banking business model became both discursively and economically increasingly discredited following the high-profile collapse of the US investment bank Lehman Brothers in September 2008. Moreover, banking business models increasingly found themselves in the media and political spotlight. For example, in the UK, the Turner Review into the banking and financial crisis called for greater regulatory scrutiny of banks in the wake of the crisis, and a limit on remuneration for bankers whose activities were deemed to pose a risk to the banking system as a whole (FSA, 2009). Meanwhile, John Vickers chaired the Independent Commission on Banking which reported to the UK government in September 2011 and argued for organisational ring fences within large banks to separate the so-called casino functions of investment banking from the utility functions of retail banking. The findings of this commission fed into the Banking Reform Act (2013), which brought in such a ring fence and was part of a wider regulatory response in the UK to the financial crisis, and which also involved the creation in April 2013 of new regulatory bodies (the Financial Conduct Authority and the Prudential Regulation Authority) that both replaced the Financial Services Authority.

For a while these changes pointed to the possibility of a radical rethinking of the power of financial services and the City of London in particular within the UK and internationally. Indeed, bankers especially found themselves in the media spotlight with attention focused particularly on their remuneration packages and especially their bonuses. However, what is remarkable is the way in which the City of London has in effect reinvented itself following the financial crisis. Perhaps this should not be so surprising given that questions can be asked concerning the true significance of the regulatory changes that were brought in following the financial crisis. For instance, John Vickers, who led the Independent Commission on Banking, is himself a previous member of the Bank of England's Monetary Policy Committee, thereby demonstrating the enduring cultural influence of the Bank and its preference for soft-touch regulation within London's financial district. The rejuvenation of London's financial district is reflected in figures on issues such as employment. For example, 2.1 million people were employed in financial services in the UK in 2012–2013, close to the total of 2.19 million that were employed before the 2007–2008 crisis (TheCityUK, 2015).

However, what these figures hide are the ways in which the types of activity within the City of London have changed following the financial crisis. Initially, the growing international make-up of financial institutions in London from the 1990s onwards had relatively little effect on the working practices of wholesale bankers, and work tended to focus on established (US) investment banking activities through corporate finance activities, particularly offering advice to corporations on mergers and acquisitions. This work was supported by investment banks making loans to their clients in order to facilitate their M&A activities. Revenue for banks in this business model was generated by charging fees for M&A advice, usually at around 1.5 per cent of the value of the deal being considered (Folkman et al., 2007). In so doing, despite the arrival of more overseas banks in London's financial district, this business model echoed in many ways that of merchant banks that had previously dominated in the City of London where banking was typically based on long-term relationships between clients and their banks, with clients usually using one bank for all their requirements rather than different banks for different types of services (Hall, 2009).

However, during the late 1990s and 2000s the profitability of this business model was challenged, primarily because more banks became involved in just one deal, thereby reducing the fee paid to any one bank (Hall, 2007). As a result, investment banks in London in the 2000s developed alternative business practices, particularly new, high-margin activities including 'trading and principal investment where the investment banker typically manages the investment bank's own account dealing in even more arcane coupons or undertakes asset management' (Folkman et al., 2007: 563). As a result, they can be understood as a form of financialised elite 'who play a significant role in shaping processes of financialisation by not simply servicing the financial and banking requirements of large corporations but also increasingly by operating in financial markets in their own right' (Hall, 2009: 179).

This shift has led to a marked change in the working practices of London's financial district banking community. Previously, investment banking was a relationship-based business as banks worked to develop long-term relationships with commercial clients. However, during the late 1990s the nature of investment banking itself changed because, for example, undertaking an M&A transaction increasingly involved not only a bilateral relationship between a bank and a corporate client, but also centred on managing the relationships between a number of financial institutions including corporate finance boutiques, hedge funds and corporate law firms, all of whom have become increasingly important in delivering the increasingly complex financial advice demanded by corporate clients (Folkman et al., 2007; Hall, 2007).

These working practices within investment banks changed even more markedly through the rise of structured finance, particularly securitisation, during the 2000s. This form of financial services work led to growing demand for individuals who were highly numerate, often holding postgraduate degrees in subjects such as maths, physics and computer science, so that these individuals could perform 'socio-financial engineering' (Pryke and Allen, 2000) in which complex structured finance products were produced that offered 'the allure of high potential margins at a corporate level and personal remuneration through bonuses at the individual level' (Hall, 2009: 184). This change in working culture, which is typified by a greater emphasis on technical and quantitative know-how rather than relation-based services, has been widely identified and debated, not least in terms of how it in part caused the international financial crisis. This demonstrates how, in addition to identifying IFCs in and of themselves, it is also important to examine the working practices that take place within them, since it is through such practices that they come to play an important role in shaping the international financial system, in times of both financial growth and financial crisis.

CONCLUSIONS

This chapter has focused on the distinctive spatial form of the international financial system in which, despite the growing use of technology and the increased mobility of knowledge and financial products and services, finance remains concentrated in a small number of IFCs. Drawing on the extensive academic literature that has developed in charting the development of these IFCs, in particular the analysis has concentrated on the case of London to show how focusing on individuals working within financial services, their working practices and their labour markets provides an instructive lens to make three main arguments. First, such a focus helps us to understand why and how IFCs remain vitally important within the international financial system. In particular, this approach helps to shed light on how such IFCs have reinvented themselves in the wake of the financial crisis, despite such centres looking very vulnerable and being sites of considerable political, media and public debate. Second, focusing on individuals also reveals how this reinvention has been based on a rather different set of activities compared with those that dominated in the finance-led boom of the 2000s. In particular, while the 2000s were dominated by large multinational banking brands, following the financial crisis these activities have increasingly been accompanied by a range of other financial services activities, notably in the form of hedge funds, pension funds and other forms of investment.

The third valuable insight that can be gained from focusing on the working practices of highly skilled financiers is that it reveals the ways in which the distinctive working cultures associated with different financial services arise through the relationship between regulatory change and financial services activity. In this respect, a greater focus on the practices of financiers, as called for within a cultural economy approach to money and finance (as they become grounded in specific institutional, regulatory and social spaces), is particularly useful. In so doing, while IFCs are vitally important to the operation of the international financial system, it is important to acknowledge the distinct make-up of financial services that comprise each centre and the distinctive working cultures and knowledge networks that underpin this. Examining the formation and transformation of these working cultures, as the analysis above has done for the case of London, is important in order to understand the continued variegated nature of the international financial system and its transformation over time.

KEY FURTHER READINGS

Leyshon, A. and Thrift, N. (1997) *Money/Space: Geographies of Monetary Transformation*. London: Routledge.
This book provides a comprehensive overview of the development of the new international financial system.

Wójcik, D. (2012) The end of investment bank capitalism? An economic geography of financial jobs and power. *Economic Geography*, 88(4): 345–368.
This paper provides a detailed analysis of the rise of the securities industry and its implications for New York's international financial district.

3

EMERGING FINANCIAL CENTRES AND THE CHANGING BALANCE OF POWER WITHIN INTERNATIONAL FINANCE

INTERNATIONAL FINANCIAL CENTRES BEYOND EUROPE AND NORTH AMERICA

Following the 2007–2008 financial crisis, there has been a growing sense in political, media, regulatory, popular and academic circles that the axis of power within the international financial system is beginning to shift eastwards. In particular, there has been a growing interest in the possibility that the Chinese currency, the renminbi (RMB), could challenge the US dollar as the dominant reserve currency in the global economy. Prior to 2004, trading denominated in RMB was not permitted outside mainland China. This meant that the Chinese currency had virtually no international influence. However, this position has changed markedly in recent years. This follows the broader internationalisation and opening up of the Chinese economy, marked most clearly by its entry into the World Trade Organization in 2001. These developments are underpinned by a desire among Chinese policy makers to reduce their country's reliance on the US dollar following the 2007-2008 financial crisis. Evidence of the growing importance of the Chinese currency internationally can be found in its inclusion in the International Monetary Fund's basket of reserve currencies (IMF, 2015). Meanwhile, in terms of the growing importance of Chinese financial institutions, in spring 2015 the Chinese government announced that the Asian Infrastructure Investment Bank (AIIB) would be created in order to stimulate infrastructure investment in the Asian region. This development is significant because it marked the addition of an Asian-led multilateral financial institution. This is in contrast to the Western-led multilateral institutions, notably the IMF and the World Bank, that have played a central role in shaping and governing the international financial system following their establishment under the post-Second-World-War Bretton Woods Agreement (see Chapter 2).

Despite these significant developments, it is important to note that there is nothing inevitable or certain about the ability of the Chinese RMB to challenge the US dollar as the global reserve currency because the growing international importance of the RMB is not a straightforward process. Indeed, as Chapter 2 demonstrated, London and New York remain the most dominant financial centres. Moreover, the history of these financial centres is marked by episodes in which their dominance appeared to be challenged largely unsuccessfully. For instance, following the financial crisis, a number of media reports suggested that hedge funds and private equity firms in particular would leave London for offshore centres, especially Zurich, in order to escape what was perceived by financiers as an increasingly draconian regulatory environment (see Chapter 5). However, the extent to which these threats to leave London have been carried out is limited. Many commentators suggest that the threats are aimed primarily at changing the regulatory environment in London to make it more favourable for financial services activity, rather than reflecting a genuine desire to leave London on the part of financial institutions.

While acknowledging the continued importance of established financial centres, it is clear that a series of new and potentially significant changes are taking place in financial centres beyond Europe and North America that need to be understood if we are to understand fully the dynamic nature of the contemporary international financial system. This chapter examines these changes through financial centres both within and beyond mainland China that are central to the internationalisation of the Chinese currency.

In so doing, the chapter responds to one of the major criticisms of cultural economy research on finance: that is, it has focused on the heartlands of global finance throughout its development in the 2000s (namely North America and Western Europe). In many ways, this geographical focus is not surprising given that these were the most important centres for financial growth at the time, both through the volume of financial transactions conducted there (see Chapter 2) and in terms of the significant financial innovations that took place such as the development of securitised finance. However, events following the crisis demonstrate the need to extend our analyses beyond these sites because this dominance is increasingly being called into question, and the experiences of different places to both the financial boom of the 2000s and the ensuing crisis are highly variegated across space.

This echoes calls to reflect more carefully on the situated nature of knowledge production within much of the social science research on money and finance that remains focused on Europe and North America (Pollard and Samers, 2007; Yeung and Lin, 2003) and particularly the need to develop more 'cosmopolitan financial geographies' (Pollard and Samers, 2013). Building on these arguments, the analysis in this chapter examines how our understandings of the making of financial market making in IFCs can be enhanced by broadening the geographical focus of research beyond a focus on the dollar, sterling and euro in North America and Western Europe. Most notably, by focusing on the Chinese currency both within and beyond China, the chapter demonstrates the need to pay more attention to the role of the state and financial regulation in processes of financial market making than has typically been the case within cultural economy research on money and finance.

The chapter develops these arguments over three further sections before concluding. First, the chapter documents the need to decentre accounts of IFCs beyond those in Western Europe and North America. Second, the chapter examines how this has been achieved to date through a focus on the changing role of financial centres associated with the shifting eastwards towards Asia of the geo-economic and geo-political power of the international financial system. Finally, the chapter examines the case of the development of Chinese financial services and the ways in which these are not only contributing to the growing power of China within global finance, but also becoming increasingly important in shaping IFCs in Europe and North America as part of wider efforts to internationalise the Chinese currency, the RMB.

MAKING FINANCIAL MARKETS BEYOND THE GLOBAL NORTH

The need to correct the dominance of research in Europe and North America within cultural economy research on money and finance is clearly demonstrated by considering the commonly used term 'the global financial crisis'. In fact, the 2007–2008 financial crisis has been a far more geographically variegated phenomenon than the term 'global' would suggest, with different countries experiencing the fallout from the crisis in different ways, as well as different regions experiencing the crisis differently (Claessens et al., 2010). For example, within Europe the plight of Greece, Portugal, Spain and Ireland has been very different to the core of the EU, particularly Germany, following the crisis (French et al., 2011). Figure 3.1 illustrates this by comparing the competitiveness of Southern European countries with Germany and the Netherlands in what is often termed the northern core

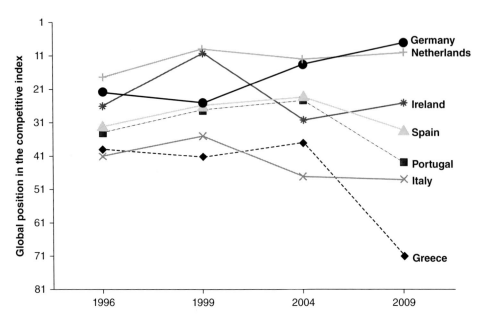

FIGURE 3.1   COMPARISON OF COMPETITIVENESS OF SOUTHERN EUROPEAN STATES, 1996-2009

Source: Hadjimichalis (2011) Geneceperro conest, quiatur ibeat.

of Europe. The figure shows how uneven development characterised the eurozone before the 2007–2008 crisis and that this geography was exacerbated by the crisis itself. Meanwhile, within-country differences are also stark. For example, house prices have grown in highly uneven ways in the run-up to the crisis in the USA and UK and have been associated with the uneven consequences of the collapse in house prices and other economic indicators following the crisis (Martin, 2011). For example, figures show that 130,000 jobs were lost in the UK in financial services between December 2007 and December 2009, while the equivalent figure for manufacturing was 1 million, which was disproportionately focused on the north and midland regions of the UK, particularly the West Midlands (Martin, 2011). This has led to a highly uneven response to the financial crisis across the UK, with peripheral regions in the north suffering declines in output and employment rates greater than those in London and the south east (see Table 3.1). This has given rise to growing academic interest in the notion of resilient regions and the ways in which different place-based assets help regions react to economic transformation and crisis (see the special issue of the *Cambridge Journal of Regions, Economy and Society* in 2010).

Such empirical developments call into question the commonly used term of a 'global financial crisis' and signal the situated nature of much of the research conducted into the international financial system. This is particularly true of cultural economy research into money and finance that, as briefly noted in Chapter 1, has focused particularly on the heartlands of global finance in London, Chicago and Wall Street. In many ways this focus can be explained by the timing and location of

TABLE 3.1 THE UNEVEN REGIONAL IMPACT OF RECESSION IN THE UK

	Output 2008 (quarter 1)–2009 (quarter 2) Percentage change	Employment 2008 (quarter 1)–2009 (quarter 2) Percentage change
London	−4.8	−1.9
South East	−4.9	−2.9
Eastern	−4.8	1.3
South West	−5.0	−2.5
West Midlands	−8.2	−3.4
East Midlands	−7.6	−4.4
Yorks–Humber	−7.3	−3.5
North West	−6.7	−2.3
North East	−8.6	−3.6
Wales	−6.9	−1.8
Scotland	−4.7	−2.4
Ireland	−5.3	NA

Source: Martin, R. 'The local geographies of the financial crisis: from the housing bubble to economic recession and beyond', *Journal of Economic Geography* (2011) 11(4): 587–618 by permission of Oxford University Press.

the development of cultural economy approaches to money and finance themselves. This literature developed predominately in the 2000s in what was a finance-led boom and a period of significant innovation in financial services through products related to particular financial technologies such as securitisation, asset-backed securities and collateralised debt obligations (Hall, 2011). Although the consequences of these financial products in terms of their role in causing the financial crisis are now well known (Wainwright, 2009; 2015), at the time research within the cultural economy approaches to money and finance focused on the heartlands of the production of these financial products, particularly in the financial districts of London and New York, rather than their outcomes in terms of wider processes of uneven economic development. For example, and reflecting the emphasis in cultural economy research placed on a range of different actors within finance beyond financiers, research has examined the role of particular financial instruments such as credit default swaps in facilitating the sub-prime mortgage market in the USA (MacKenzie, 2012). Further, work has also interrogated the way in which the use of specific modelling approaches within investment banks, particularly in the USA, was a critical element in the collapse of the investment banking business model in the immediate aftermath of the crisis (MacKenzie and Spears, 2014a; 2014b). Indeed, this concern with understanding the processes of innovation within leading financial markets has continued within cultural economy research following the crisis through emerging work on the development of high-speed trading (see MacKenzie et al., 2012).

However, the variegated experiences of different cities, regions and countries, in terms of both causing and responding to the financial crisis, demand that cultural economy research acknowledges the partiality of academic accounts of money and finance that are produced through a limited number of research sites. Within work

on money and finance more generally, this has led to calls to decentre our understanding of money and finance by broadening the geographical locations studied
and in turn the types of financial services and markets analysed (Pollard et al., 2009;
Pollard and Samers, 2007). For example, Pollard et al. (2009: 138) argue in the
case of the development of postcolonial perspectives in economic geography that
research needs to 'examine how and where economic practices and theories travel
… [and emphasise] the importance of exploring "domestication"', something that
is beginning to be picked up in research into the internationalisation of service
firms beyond the case of finance (see for example Boussebaa et al., 2012). Such an
approach would not only examine the development of financial products in North
America for example, but also study how such products change or are used differently as they travel to different financial markets, as well as examining what we can
learn about finance by studying its production in places beyond North America and
Western Europe.

DECENTRING ACCOUNTS OF MONEY AND FINANCE

One body of research that has sought to decentre accounts of money and finance
beyond the established IFCs is social scientific work on Islamic finance and specifi-
cally the intersection between this and 'western' finance. At root, Islamic banking
and finance (IBF) can be understood as the provision of a range of financial services
that comply with the beliefs and regulatory frameworks of Islam, and particularly
sharia law (Pollard and Samers, 2007). Two key elements of this framing of IBF mean
that it departs from 'western' finance in important ways. First, *riba*, or interest, is not
allowed to be charged on money lending. Instead, while 'the provider of capital is
not permitted to fix a pre-determined rate of interest, [they] should be allowed an
adequate return by having a financial stake in the project being undertaken' (Pollard
and Samers, 2007: 314). Second, excessive risk taking is also prohibited, so investments are not generally permitted in activities such as gambling and other activities
that are not seen as being desirable within Islam, such as businesses with links to
alcohol. These rules mean that money within IBF is much more closely entwined
with the 'real economy' rather than being used as a source of speculation and income
in its own right (see also Maurer, 2005). Indeed, as Table 3.2 demonstrates, the sharia-
compliant governance of IBF gives rise to distinct contractual relations that shape
both the nature of Islamic banking and financial systems and their relationship with
the wider economy.

Work on IBF demonstrates that this sector has grown significantly over the last
20 years. However, although growth rates are particularly impressive in Islamic states,
a key finding of research on IBF is the growing intersection between Islamic and
mainstream western finance. This can be seen in measures of the importance of different financial centres within IBF. Table 3.3 shows the ranking of such centres based
on their connectivity with other Islamic financial centres, their clustering of service
sector activities and the number of headquarter offices of the leading 500 Islamic
financial institutions located in the city.

TABLE 3.2 EXAMPLES OF COMMON ISLAMIC FINANCE CONTRACTUAL FORMS

Name of contract	Approximate equivalent	Technique
Ijara wa iqtina	Lease-to-purchase	Borrower pays rent based on equity share (initially determined by down payment) plus predetermined and unchanging portion of the principal. With each payment to the principal, borrower's equity share increases, and so rent decreases. Rent determined by making to market
Istisna'a	Manufacturing partnership	Finance company funds construction of a house, factory or business, or the purchase of a piece of equipment, for the borrower, then purchases through ijara or other process
Mudarabah	Limited partnership	Borrower and finance company enter into limited partnership and form a corporate entity; borrower rents from the corporate entity, increasing borrower's share in entity over time until it is completely owned by the borrower. The object of the contract is the corporate partnership itself, which over time is bought out by the borrower
Murabaha (bai bi thamin al ajil)	Deferred payment sale	Borrower pays finance company, which holds title until complete payoff of principal plus administration costs
Musharaka	Joint venture	Similar to mudarabah, but finance company and borrower share title as 'co-owners' of the property rather than as partners in a separate corporate entity. The objects of the contract is the property, not the corporate partnership

Source: Maurer (2005: 41)

Republished with permission of Princeton University Press, from *Mutual Life, Limited: Islamic Banking, Alternative Currencieson, Lateral Reason*, Maurer, 2005, p. 41; permission conveyed through Copyright Clearance Center, Inc.

TABLE 3.3 TOP 20 RANKED ISLAMIC FINANCIAL SERVICE CENTRES

Rank	City
1	Manama
2	Tehran
3	London
4	Dubai
5	Amman
6	Beirut
7	Paris
8	Istanbul
9	Abu Dhabi
10	Cairo
11	Tunis
12	Kuala Lumpur
13	Algiers
14	Baghdad
15	Jeddah
16	Al Ain
17	Karachi
18	Muscat
19	Ras-Al-Khaimah
20	New York

Source: Adapted from Bassens et al. (2010: 43)

Republished with permission of John Wiley & Sons Inc, adapted from 'Searching for the Mecca of finance: Islamic financial services and the world city network', Bassens et al., *Area*, 42(1), 2010; permission conveyed through Copyright Clearance Center, Inc.

One implication of this research is to demonstrate the importance of financial centres beyond the 'usual suspects' of New York and London through a form of finance that is rarely studied. In the case of IBF, this points to the importance of the Gulf region and the ways in which this serves to reproduce existing power relations within global finance more generally (Bassens, 2012). However, the relationship between western finance and IBF also demonstrates the value of decentring accounts of money and finance beyond the Global North, because it sheds theoretical light on how contemporary global finance involves the intersection between the mobility of money, people and practices on the one hand, and the territorial qualities of financial centres on the other.

This can be seen through a focus on the sharia scholars who are central to determining what counts as a legitimate practice within Islamic finance but who do not sit neatly within existing frameworks for understanding the (re)production of financial elites within mainstream financial centres (compare Pollard and Samers (2013) with Hall and Appleyard (2009) and Faulconbridge and Hall (2014), for example). These scholars are experts in Islamic law and are typically appointed to the boards of Islamic banks to ensure their activities are sharia compliant. Further, this research demonstrates how these individuals embody a cosmopolitan subjectivity that combines social and religious beliefs learnt through Islam with the regulatory landscapes in which they operate in the west as Islamic finance continues to grow in the heartlands of global finance, notably the USA and UK. In so doing, research on Islamic finance demonstrates the value of studying finance beyond the Global North, not only in terms of enhancing understandings of important developments within the international financial system, such as the rise of specialist Islamic banking and financial centres, but also to show how understanding these developments can enhance theoretical understandings of global finance in both established and emerging markets because there is no neat separation between 'mainstream' and 'Islamic' finance.

CHALLENGING THE DOMINANCE OF WESTERN FINANCIAL CENTRES

The dominance of London and New York as IFCs is relatively well established and demonstrated through the consultancy industry that has developed to rank financial centres across a range of factors, including regulatory environment and labour force characteristics (see for example those published by Z/Yen). However, beyond North America and Europe, the importance of different financial centres is more fluid (Aalbers, 2009a). This is reflected in research that identifies and specifies the changing relationships between a small number of leading cities that act as key nodes in choreographing the global economy and the international financial system in particular. This work has been led by the Globalisation and World Cities (GaWC) Group at Loughborough University, and although New York and London are shown to be the dominant centres in North America and Europe, early work in Asia showed that Hong Kong, Singapore and Tokyo all played an important role in shaping the regional economy (Taylor, 2001). This work builds on a wider literature that documents the importance of knowledge-intensive, advanced producer firms such as finance, law and advertising for the creation of significant economic clusters inside a small number of global cities that act as 'command and control' centres within the global economy (Sassen, 2001 [1991]). Methodologically, this research began by identifying those cities that contained the largest clusters of headquarter offices of transnational corporations (Beaverstock et al., 2000).

However, more recent work has refined this methodology to assess the importance of cities in the global economy by examining the headquarter office location of advanced business service firms (which includes accountancy, finance, insurance, legal and management consultancy firms) (Beaverstock et al., 2002; Taylor, 2001). This research argues that there are a relatively small number of cities that host clusters of these activities and that become important settings for: the production of innovation; the sharing of new knowledge concerning development in for example financial products; and the centre of associated highly skilled labour markets (in the case of financial services, see for example Thrift, 1994). This approach, as illustrated in Table 3.4, has begun to point to the changing dynamics of global cities, and IFCs in particular, by signalling the relative decline of Tokyo, the ongoing importance of Hong Kong and Singapore, and the growing significance of Beijing and Shanghai (Beaverstock et al., 2002). The case of Tokyo illustrates clearly the changing fortunes of financial centres over time (see Box 3.1). Its relative decline from the 1990s onwards can be attributed partly to growing competition from newer financial centres, discussed below, but also from the bursting of the Japanese asset price bubble in the early 1990s that had significant ramifications for the Japanese economy more generally, giving rise to the term 'the lost decade' referring to the period of economic stagnation in the 1990s (see Box 3.1).

TABLE 3.4 RANK OF LONDON AND NEW YORK AND OF ASIAN CITIES AMONG GLOBAL CITIES BY CONNECTIVITY OF THEIR BUSINESS SERVICES FIRMS IN 2000 AND 2008

2000			2008		
Rank	**City**	**% of highest**	**Rank**	**City**	**% of highest**
1	London	100	1	New York	100
2	New York	97	2	London	99
3	Hong Kong	73	3	Hong Kong	83
4	Tokyo	71	5	Singapore	76
6	Singapore	67	6	Tokyo	74
19	Taipei	48	8	Shanghai	69
20	Jakarta	48	10	Beijing	68
23	Mumbai	47	14	Seoul	63
27	Shanghai	44	17	Mumbai	59
28	Kuala Lumpur	44	18	Kula Lumpur	58
29	Beijing	43	20	Taipei	56
30	Seoul	42	28	Jakarta	53

Source: Meyer (2015: 208)

─BOX 3.1─

THE BURSTING OF THE JAPANESE BUBBLE ECONOMY

Japan is an important, but often forgotten, site of analysis for the changing fortunes of IFCs:

1   Japan enjoyed impressive economic growth rates in the 1970s and 1980s.

2   This was reflected in, at its peak, the Japanese stock market making up 42 per cent of total global market capitalisation.

3   This growth was built to a significant extent on the cheap and ready availability of credit, leading to an asset price bubble.

4   This 'bubble economy' burst in the late 1980s and early 1990s.

5   Between 1990 and 2003, the Japanese annual average rate of growth was just 1.2 per cent, with Tokyo suffering associated pressure on its position as a leading IFC.

Source: Dicken (2011)

Hong Kong and Singapore, in contrast to Tokyo, have used their importance based on their colonial connections to Europe and their reliance on expatriate labour to maintain their rankings as the fourth and third most important IFCs globally, respectively behind London and New York (see Table 2.1). However, the significance and product focus of these two centres has more recently become the subject of considerable change as the regional dynamics in Asia and the global dynamics of relationships between financial centres have become the subject of intensified debate and change following the increasingly important role played by China within the global economy and the international financial system more generally (Walter and Howie, 2011; Wu, 2000; Yusuf and Wu, 2002). As a result, Shanghai and Beijing are both developing their own financial centres as well as influencing the nature of financial services activities that take place beyond China, particularly in Singapore and London. Investigating these developments in more detail reveals the ways in which understandings of IFCs need to appreciate not only the agglomeration economy benefits within cities, but also the ways in which relations between centres are important as they seek to make new financial markets.

THE RISE OF CHINESE IFCs AND CHANGING FINANCIAL GEOGRAPHIES IN ASIA

Since its foundation in 1949, the People's Republic of China has developed a state-owned banking system modelled on that of the Soviet Union. This system was dominated by the People's Bank of China, supported by three state-owned banks

(Bank of China, Bank of Communications and Agricultural Bank of China) that provided finance to China's state-owned enterprises (Lai, 2012). This arrangement changed following the adoption of China's Open Door policy of economic reform in 1978, following which, in the 1980s, the state-owned banks were reconfigured into four banks (Bank of China, Agricultural Bank of China, China Construction Bank, and Industrial and Commercial Bank) tasked with running the commercial lending and branch networks previously operated by the PBOC. Meanwhile, PBOC itself became the central bank. As part of the wider economic reforms that were ushered in at this time, Shanghai was positioned as the 'dragonhead' of the Chinese economy, leading its increasingly international focus (Yusuf and Wu, 2002). Meanwhile, in addition to the reorganisation of China's domestic banking sector, foreign banks were encouraged to set up offices and operations in China in order to facilitate the flow of foreign capital and knowledge of innovative banking practices globally into China.

While these changes have had a significant impact on domestic banking within China, they also demonstrate the ways in which Chinese IFCs are tied into global financial networks. Indeed, these networks are both shaping and being shaped by the transformation of the Chinese banking sector and its associated IFCs. For example, three sets of actors have been central in creating networks between Chinese and international IFCs that have been important in shaping the transformation of Shanghai and Beijing (Lai, 2012):

1   'Regulatory learning partners': This refers to the signing of bilateral Regulatory Cooperation Memorandums of Understanding between the Chinese monetary authorities, particularly the Chinese Banking Regulatory Commission (CBRC), and a number of international regulatory counterparts in a range of countries including the USA, UK, Canada, Hong Kong and Singapore. The relationship with the UK has been particularly close: the UK's Financial Services Authority (FSA) was a particularly attractive regulatory body as a model for China's developing regulatory landscape, partly because of the close relationship fostered through the western educational backgrounds of senior officials in the CBRC with the UK's regulatory community and practices.

2   Individual experts: A small number of individuals were also particularly important in facilitating the circulation and translation of western financial practices into China. Special attention has been paid in encouraging successful Chinese financiers who have experience working in other financial centres to return to China (Zweig, 2006).

3   Market actors: Key financial institutions, particularly the newly arrived international banks in Chinese IFCs, have been important in facilitating the flow of knowledge and information into China's banking system, particularly through 'aligning the Chinese industry with the latest developments in global banking market' (CBRC, 2007, cited in Lai, 2011: 102) in areas such as banking provision to small and medium-sized enterprises, which had not been a historically important market for Chinese state-owned banks.

In addition to facilitating the greater participation of Chinese institutions in the global financial system, these developments have also shaped the relations between Chinese financial centres and the wider international financial system. Historically, work on Asian financial centres has demonstrated that both Beijing and Shanghai have lagged some way behind Hong Kong and Singapore as the leading financial centres in Asia (see Taylor, 2006). However, more recent work has shown how Shanghai and Beijing have sought to develop their financial centre competiveness, albeit in different ways. Building on its identification as a strategically important city for the development of the Yangtze Delta region and its more outward-facing nature in relation to the global economy, Shanghai has been the leading location of choice for foreign banks in China. However, Beijing hosts the key regulatory functions of China's financial infrastructure including, most notably, the headquarters of the state-owned banks, the PBOC, the China Banking Regulatory Commission and the State Administration of Foreign Exchange.

As a result, these two cities are essentially making different kinds of financial markets, with some even questioning the ongoing dominance of Shanghai in financial services (see Zhao, 2003 for example, and Lai, 2012). These changes are reflected in the headquarter location of foreign banks in China. Those international banks that are aiming to service multinational corporations in China, such as Goldman Sachs and Morgan Stanley, typically locate their headquarters in Shanghai, while those that prioritise developing a close dialogue with the regulatory and monetary authorities in Beijing typically locate there, such as HSBC and Standard Chartered (Lai, 2012). These different strategies for financial centres are reflected elsewhere in Asia. For example, Singapore and Hong Kong are also increasingly pursuing different strategies in order to maintain their position as leading international financial centres. Singapore is increasingly focused on asset and fund management as private wealth in Asia locates there. Meanwhile, Hong Kong is seeking to use its unique position as a Special Administrative Region to act as a full-service financial centre that connects mainland China with the rest of the international financial system. Indeed, this connection has increasingly become two way in nature as China has sought not only to open up its domestic banking and financial services markets, but also to facilitate the internationalisation of its banks in the broader financial system.

MAKING CHINESE BANKING MARKETS BEYOND MAINLAND CHINA

While the growing power of Chinese IFCs has drawn on the broader global financial networks of which it is a part, the transformation of Chinese banking and financial services also has important implications for the nature of global finance beyond the boundaries of mainland China. Examining this ongoing transformation is important empirically because the Chinese currency, the RMB, is becoming an increasingly significant actor within international finance, yet existing cultural economy research has not considered this type of financial market. Theoretically, studying the growing importance of Chinese banking and financial services beyond the borders of mainland China is important because it demonstrates the limitations of developing understandings of global finance predominately through studies of established IFCs, notably in North America and Western Europe. In particular, it reveals the important role of the Chinese state, particularly the financial and monetary authorities in Beijing, in shaping the transformation of the Chinese banking system. In so doing, it places questions of state and regulatory power much more centrally in analyses of the international financial system, elements that have been comparatively neglected within extant cultural economy research on finance (Hall, 2011).

UNDERSTANDING RMB INTERNATIONALISATION AND THE ROLE OF IFCs BEYOND MAINLAND CHINA - THE RISE OF OFFSHORE RMB CENTRES

China's desire to internationalise its currency has been described as the 'most significant global financial markets development since the formation of the Euro' (Deutsche Bank, 2014: 2). There is no clear starting date for this process of internationalisation, although it builds on China's wider 'going out' policy that was established in 1999 and, among other things, seeks to encourage strategically important state-owned firms, known as 'national champions', to increase their international operations. Building on this broader political agenda, a number of policy changes have been made by political and financial authorities in Beijing to facilitate the internationalisation of the RMB from the early 2000s onwards (Chen and Cheung, 2011; Walter and Howie, 2011). For example, a key document in RMB internationalisation entitled 'The timing, path and strategies of RMB internationalization' was published by the PBOC (PBOC Study Group, 2006). This document supported the currency internationalisation of the RMB because it argued that this process could support and improve the wider competitiveness of the Chinese economy. Moreover, amid supporting claims that there were multiple, country and regionally specific experiences of the 2007–2008 financial crisis, the Chinese government became a more enthusiastic supporter of RMB internationalisation after the crisis as China sought to reduce its reliance on the US dollar for trade purposes in an effort to shield its economy from future crises (Walter and Howie, 2011; Zhang, 2009). In the early phases of RMB internationalisation, policy attention focused on supporting the further internationalisation of Chinese trade by increasing the use of the RMB in international trade settlements, particularly through the Cross-Border RMB Trade Settlement Scheme launched in 2009. Building on this, RMB internationalisation has increasingly focused on positioning the RMB as a key currency and financial asset in its own right.

This has been achieved through a distinctively spatial organisation of policies aimed at internationalisation. In particular, the Chinese government has aimed to manage and control RMB internationalisation carefully through a gradual process of capital account liberalisation while maintaining control of exchange rates

(He and McCauley, 2010). As a result, a distinctive pattern of regulatory reform and RMB internationalisation has emerged in which there is a separation between onshore RMB markets in mainland China on the one hand (using the currency designation CNY), in which interest and exchange rates remain in place, and offshore markets on the other hand (using the currency designation CNH), in which interest and exchange rates have been deregulated.

The use of offshore spaces is particularly interesting because it is through these spaces that the influence of Chinese currency internationalisation is being felt within global finance more generally. In this respect, a small but growing network of offshore RMB networks has been created. These offshore RMB centres are defined as financial centres 'outside [mainland] China that conduct a wide variety of financial services denominated in RMB' (ASIFMA, 2014: 20). Hong Kong became the first such centre in mid-2010, reflecting its position as an experimental site for Chinese economic reform as part of its role as a Chinese Special Administrative Area (Chen and Cheung, 2011; Walter and Howie, 2011). However, a growing number of additional centres have been created, focused initially in Asia and including Singapore and Taipei but becoming increasingly global in nature, including cities such as Toronto, Luxembourg and London. Within this network, Hong Kong, London and Singapore have emerged as the most significant centres with the densest networks of RMB-related financial services including RMB-denominated deposits, a swap line directly with Beijing and a related RMB-denominated financial infrastructure including Chinese banks and an RMB clearing bank (see Table 3.5).

TABLE 3.5 FINANCIAL FUNCTION AND DEVELOPMENT OF OFFSHORE RMB CENTRES

Financial function	Hong Kong	Singapore	Taiwan	London
RMB deposits (bn) (date)	944 (Sept. 2014)	254 (June 2014)	300 (Sept. 2014)	25 (Dec. 2014)
Clearing bank	Bank of China Hong Kong	ICBC SG	BOC TW	China Construction Bank
RQFII quota (bn) (date of initial allocation)	270 (2011)	50 (2013)	100 (proposed)	80 (2014)
RMB swap line (bn) (entry date)	400 (2014)	300 (2013)	NA	200 (2013)
Competitive advantages	Largest offshore RMB centre, unique geo-political relationship with mainland China, experimental site for new RMB liberalisation policies	Important ASEAN trading hub, key Chinese investment partner, global asset management centre	Regionally important trading centre with China	Leading international financial centre, strategically important geographical and time zone location, growing experience in RMB financial services

Sources: Adapted from Hall (2017) using author's research and PwC (2015); adapted from Huang (2015)

LONDON'S DEVELOPMENT AS AN OFFSHORE RMB CENTRE

The development of London as an offshore RMB centre is an important case study because it is the 'offshore renminbi centre of choice in the west' in the words of Wenjian Fang, Chief Executive of Bank of China London (Euromoney, 2014). However, it is important to remember that the presence of Chinese financial institutions in London's financial district is not solely a function of the development as an offshore RMB centre. For example, Bank of China opened an affiliate office in London in 1929. Nevertheless, since 2011 there has been a concerted effort by financial and political authorities in both London and Beijing to develop London's functions as an offshore RMB centre, following a meeting between the Chinese Vice Premier, Wang Qishan, and UK Chancellor, George Osborne, at which they publicly stated their commitment to London as such a centre. Although Table 3.5 shows that London remains a smaller offshore RMB centre in terms of numbers of activities and size of RMB deposits, it is its geo-political significance as the first and leading western offshore RMB centre that is particularly important to study in terms of revealing how RMB internationalisation is shaping IFCs beyond the borders of mainland China.

One way of advancing understandings of London's development in this respect is to focus on the Chinese banking sector and the entry of Chinese banks into London. Following the wider process of going out (discussed above), the internationalisation of Chinese banking has been spearheaded by what are known as the 'Big Four' state-owned commercial banks (Bank of China, Agricultural Bank of China, China Construction Banking Corporation, Industrial and Commercial Bank of China). Indeed, under this policy all four of these banks have increased their overseas operations. Subsequently, significant milestones have been passed in Chinese bank internationalisation. Perhaps most notably, Industrial and Commercial Bank of China (ICBC) was the first Chinese bank to be ranked first in The Banker's Top 1000, and all of the Chinese 'Big Four' banks are ranked within the top 10 by Tier 1 capital.

Two phases of Chinese bank internationalisation can be identified. The first phase from the early 2000s onwards was underpinned by a strategy of 'following the customer' into international markets. This reflected the broader opening up of the Chinese economy in which state-owned firms were also being encouraged to expand their operations following China's entry into the World Trade Organization in 2002. Chinese banks were well placed with their specific knowledge of how to service the distinctive requirements of these internationalising Chinese firms. The organisational form of this stage of internationalisation was dominated by mergers and particularly the acquisition of domestic banks in important trading regions with China, especially South Asia, Africa and the Americas. ICBC has followed this strategy most strongly with figures suggesting that it has spent US$7 billion in international acquisitions. Notably, it became the first Chinese bank to operate within the USA retail banking market through its acquisition of 13 branches in California and New York from the Bank of East Asia for US$140 million.

Building on this early focus on trade and subsequently retail finance, the second phase of Chinese bank internationalisation covers the 2010s onwards and is associated with the role of internationalising Chinese banks within the broader processes of RMB internationalisation. It was at this point that the internationalisation strategy moved beyond its regional focus and became increasingly concerned with opening branches, usually through organic office opening rather than merger and acquisition, in offshore RMB centres. In the case of Europe, this resulted in the European headquarters of the 'Big Four' state banks being opened in Luxembourg, reflecting its position as an important asset management centre. However, the case of London is particularly interesting since, despite having a well-established Chinese retail banking presence, and being recognised as a leading international financial centre with particular strengths in foreign exchange markets, the internationalisation of wholesale banking has, historically at least, lagged behind that of Luxembourg.

Importantly, the initial opening up of London as a financial centre for the location of Chinese banks was facilitated to a large extent by the political and monetary authorities in both London and particularly Beijing. This is significant because much of the literature on firms' internationalisation, including that of banks, has documented how bank internationalisation often takes place as banks follow their corporate clients into new markets, as happened with the internationalisation of Japanese banks into the UK in the 1990s (Tickell, 1994). However, following the financial crisis, the ability of Chinese banks to open branches in London was restricted because, at that time, overseas banks in the UK could only have subsidiaries rather than branches. This was because the UK regulatory authorities favoured subsidiaries as they were seen as less risky and have higher liquidity requirements than bank branches. Partly in response to this, London appeared to be losing out to Luxembourg as the leading European offshore RMB centre, since Luxembourg actively encouraged the opening of Chinese bank branches, with the European headquarters of the Chinese 'Big Four' banks opening in Luxembourg rather than London. Moreover, diplomatic relations between China and the UK deteriorated significantly following the meeting between Prime Minister David Cameron and the Dalai Llama in April 2012, making it even less likely that Chinese banks would be able to open in London. Indeed, the spokesperson for the Chinese foreign ministry at the time, Hong Lei, described the meeting as one that 'hurts the feelings of the Chinese people' (www. theguardian.com/world/2012/may/15/china-unhappy-cameron-dalai-lama).

In an effort to restore diplomatic relations and to facilitate London's development as an offshore RMB centre, a meeting was held by the Bank of England governor at the time, Mervyn King, with his Chinese counterpart in 2013, in which he sought to use financial services as a tool to improve geo-political relations. Importantly for the focus of this chapter, following this meeting, the UK's Prudential Regulatory Authority stated that it would consider applications for Chinese banks to open branches rather than subsidiaries in London. This commitment was formalised in October 2013 at a meeting between the Chinese Vice Premier, Ma Kai, and the UK's Chancellor of the Exchequer, George Osborne. The first Chinese bank to be given such a licence was Industrial and Commercial Bank of China, which obtained its full UK banking licence in London at the end of 2014 and was then closely followed by the other 'Big Four' state-owned banks.

However, while the Chinese state authorities in particular have been central to facilitating the initial market entry of Chinese banks into London, their continued role in shaping the process of bank internationalisation has limited the ability of Chinese state-owned banks to develop their activities in London. The resulting organisational form of Chinese banks in London can be understood as 'banking with Chinese characteristics' (Hall, 2015), which includes the banks' choice of location, the way in which they continue to try to shape demand for their services in London, and their staffing policies:

- In terms of location, all of the 'Big Four' banks are located extremely close to the Bank of England. This resembles the location of banks in Beijing, where being close to the regulator, in this case the Bank of China, is seen as being central to learning of market developments that are relevant to future business growth.

- Second, Chinese banks have struggled to create market demand for their services in London, and this partly reflects the strong role that the Chinese state has played in their internationalisation efforts and in their approach to banking in mainland China. Recent work on the internationalisation of transnational service corporations has increasingly demonstrated that corporate internationalisation not only relies on responding to client demand in new geographical markets or following existing clients into new markets, but also focuses on stimulating demand by educating potential new customers about the value of using their services through a range of activities (see for example Faulconbridge and Muzio, 2015). The fact that Chinese bank internationalisation in London has, initially at least, been driven predominately by regulatory and political aspirations has meant that Chinese banks have not been led primarily into London through following their clients.

  However, the ability of Chinese banks to subsequently create market demand in London is limited by regulation, particularly from Beijing, associated with different understandings of how banking markets operate in the UK and China. In particular, Chinese banks operating in London continue to assume that policy interventions rather than corporate market making are central to attracting new clients. This is particularly true in terms of how clients are obtained. In China, state-owned corporations are mandated to use state-owned banks and, hence, banks are not used to developing deeper relationships with potential clients and using this to build a client base in London.

- The third element of 'banking with Chinese characteristics' relates to the staffing policies of the newly opened bank branches in London. The labour market of Chinese commercial banks in London is made up of two main groups. First, senior positions within the banks are filled through secondments from the

Chinese head office. A secondment typically lasts five years and this sets the time horizon within which these managers make decisions. As a result, these managers tend to be focused on progressing their own careers rather than trying to develop the banks' operations over a longer time frame. Meanwhile, more junior positions are filled by Chinese-born nationals, some of whom have been educated in mainland China and some of whom had come to the UK for undergraduate study and worked their way into Chinese state-owned banks' commercial divisions, often through previous work experience in their more well-established UK retail divisions. This preference for Chinese employees reflects the language requirements within Chinese banks in which staff need to be bilingual in Mandarin and English, but also reflects more general issues of working cultures in which managers feel that junior staff who are accustomed to Chinese working cultures will work better in Chinese banks. However, this flow of Chinese recruits limits the ability of Chinese banks to network effectively with domestic UK clients since they are more focused on Chinese working cultures than those of their potential clients. Moreover, the supply of such staff has increasingly come under threat as the UK government has sought to limit overseas immigration numbers as part of a wider anti-immigration discourse in UK politics. As a result, while the emergence of 'banking with Chinese characteristics' within state-owned Chinese banks in London was initially facilitated through regulatory decisions made in London and Beijing, the banks' continued growth in London has been hampered by the continued dominance of Chinese regulatory regimes on the branches operating beyond mainland China.

CONCLUSIONS

This chapter has expanded the analysis of IFCs that has developed within cultural economy approaches to money and finance. Research in this cultural economy tradition has tended to build its theoretical and empirical contribution through a focus on research in the established leading IFCs of North America and Europe. In order to move beyond this focus, the chapter has focused on two important developments that have originated beyond these heartlands of finance capitalism: first, the intersection between Islamic finance and 'western finance' that in many ways has been at the cutting edge of decentring understandings of global finance; and, second, the internationalisation of the Chinese currency, the RMB, which has been identified as one of the most important future developments within the international financial system and yet has received comparatively little academic research attention to date.

In addition to revealing how these financial systems are articulating and shaping 'mainstream' financial systems, this analysis also reveals how broadening the range of research sites used in research can add significant new insights to understandings of global finance. Two such observations stand out as being particularly important.

First, studying a range of financial systems demonstrates that these do not develop in isolation. Rather developments in one particular financial market can have important implications in other markets that are seemingly geographically distanciated. For example, the opening of Chinese bank branches in London can only be understood when regulatory changes in both the UK and China are included in the analysis. Second, the case of Chinese RMB internationalisation demonstrates the importance of attending to the power relations that shape the international financial system and the politics associated with this. In so doing, this provides one valuable way of responding to criticisms that cultural economy research has so far not engaged sufficiently with the power relations that lie at the heart of financial market making.

KEY FURTHER READINGS

Lai, K.P.Y. (2012) Differentiated markets: Shanghai, Beijing and Hong Kong in China's financial centre network. *Urban Studies*, 49(6): 1275–1296.
This paper reports on original research conducted into the changing geographies of IFCs within greater China.

Pollard, J. and Samers, M. (2007) Islamic banking and finance: postcolonial political economy and the decentring of economic geography. *Transactions of the Institute of British Geographers*, 32(3): 313–330.
This paper provides more detail concerning the value of decentring understandings of money and finance beyond a focus on North America and Western Europe.

SECTION II

SPACES OF FINANCE AND THE 'REAL' ECONOMY

4

FINANCIALISATION AND MAKING FINANCE PRODUCTIVE

Chapter summary

- Introduction
- Why do the links between finance and the 'real economy' matter?
- Financialisation: making the connections between finance and the 'real economy'
- Using networks to understand the relations between finance and the 'real economy'
- Networks and relational approaches to the global economy
  - *Firm and financial networks*
  - *Infrastructure and financial networks*
- Conclusions

INTRODUCTION

The cultural economy approach to understanding money and finance discussed in the first part of this book has been invaluable in responding to calls for research on money and finance to 'speak the language' (Leyshon, 1998: 442) of finance more fluently. Such an approach means moving beyond understanding the organisational structure of finance largely at a macro scale, and instead focuses on the detailed operations within and between financial institutions. In so doing, cultural economy approaches to money and finance have been central in identifying the constellation of different financial actors that are central to the daily operation of finance, revealing how global finance is in fact reproduced through working practices that cross-cut straightforward scalar distinctions of the global and the local. For example, cultural economy approaches are particularly interested in specifying the technical and computational infrastructures that underpin financial markets. These range from mathematical formulae to the fibre optic cable that supports high-frequency trading (MacKenzie, 2003b; 2014). These material and technological underpinnings of global finance are termed market devices (Muniesa et al., 2007) within cultural economy research. Work has also focused on a better understanding of the similarities and differences between the working cultures of particular financial institutions and banks (MacKenzie and Spears, 2014a; 2014b), as well as the characteristics of different IFCs such as London and New York as discussed in Chapter 2 (Ho, 2009; Zaloom, 2006).

However, despite the advances made in this work for our understanding of the day-to-day operation of finance, critics of cultural economy approaches to money and finance argue that by placing the detailed nature of financial markets at the centre of its analysis, cultural economy research has the potential to reify the world of high finance, portraying it as a glamorous service sector, replete with intrigue and gossip as depicted in the popular media such as the 1987 film *Wall Street* and the 2000 film *Boiler Room*. In particular, through the use of particular elements of financial theory in the (re)production of the international financial system, cultural economy research on money and finance has been criticised for its tendency to focus on how financial markets operate and the decision making that shapes this, rather than addressing the power relations that lie at the heart of the international financial system and its relationship with the rest of economic life, such that finance plays a vital role in contributing to the ongoing patterns of uneven development that characterise the world economy (Pryke and Du Gay, 2007).

However, the 2007–2008 financial crisis and the ensuing low economic growth rates in North America and Western Europe, in particular, demonstrate the need to develop more critical and politically attuned cultural economy analyses of global finance. Such an approach would pay more attention not only to the operation of finance in and of itself, but also to the implications of the nature of international finance for the wider economic livelihoods of individuals, households, firms and regions, whose everyday financial decision making can seem far removed from the centres of high finance. Furthermore, there is also a need for research on the heartlands of the international financial system – the IFCs discussed in Chapter 2 – to reflect more critically on the causes and consequences of the financial crisis.

This chapter responds to this lack of attention to the politics and power of finance within cultural economy research by focusing on the intersection between finance, financial services and the rest of the economy.

WHY DO THE LINKS BETWEEN FINANCE AND THE 'REAL ECONOMY' MATTER?

One of the leitmotifs of political and popular debate following the financial crisis across several advanced economies has been calls to 'rebalance' the economy away from finance towards the 'real' economy – typically understood as manufacturing (BIS 2010a; 2010b; 2011). For example, Peter Mandelson, in his capacity as the then

Deputy Prime Minister of the UK in 2009, reflected critically on the development of an increasing range of financial products and the growth of quantitative finance more generally in the City of London in the 2000s (Hall, 2006) by stating that economic growth demanded 'an economy with less financial engineering and more real engineering'.

The case of the UK is particularly interesting in this respect because it reveals the very clear geography associated with these processes. For example, upon taking office, the then UK Prime Minister David Cameron argued that:

> Our economy has become more and more unbalanced, with our fortunes hitched to a few industries in one corner of the country, while we let other sectors like manufacturing slide. Today our economy is heavily reliant on just a few industries and a few regions – particularly London and the South East. This really matters. An economy with such a narrow foundation for growth is fundamentally unstable and wasteful – because we are not making use of the talent out there in all parts of our United Kingdom. We are determined that should change.(Cameron, 2010, cited in Martin et al., 2015: 343)

This reflects more long-standing concerns that the financial services industry in London has developed at the expense of other regions and sectors within the UK. For example, as Figure 4.1 shows, London and the south east of England have enjoyed economic growth rates that have outpaced those of other regions for some time, and a significant factor within this has been the dominance of financial services.

Meanwhile, in the USA, this criticism has been framed as a question of power relations between Wall Street (that is, the financial services sector) and Main Street (shorthand for the 'ordinary' and 'everyday' US economy beyond the world of high finance). This debate received the most media attention following the first Occupy protest on Wall Street on 17 September 2011. Occupy has subsequently gone on to become an international movement that draws attention to the increasing income inequality between the richest in several economies in Europe and North America and the rest of the population. Indeed, this emphasis on income inequality has been given further impetus following the publication of the French economist Thomas Piketty's (2013) book *Capital in the Twenty First Century*, which takes a historical approach to examine changes in income inequality (see also Chapter 5).

However, these analyses of the relationship between financial services and the rest of the economy work, implicitly at least, with a separation between financial services and what are positioned as the more productive components of the 'real economy', such as manufacturing and trade relationships. In contrast, this chapter questions this assumption, following research that has problematised such a separation between finance and the rest of the economy (Christophers, 2011a). In order to do this, the chapter examines the value of developing more networked understandings of finance that focus precisely on the links between finance and other parts of economic life. To do this, two main bodies of research are drawn upon: first, work in relation to economic geography (see Dicken et al., 2001; Yeung, 2005); and second,

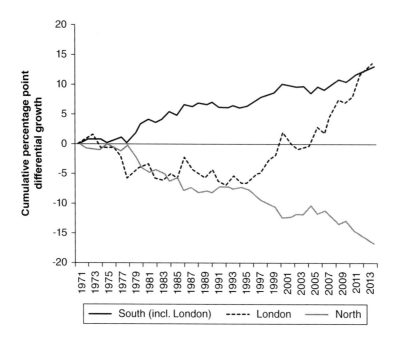

FIGURE 4.1 CUMULATIVE ANNUAL PERCENTAGE-POINT GROWTH GAPS IN GROSS VALUE ADDED (2011 PRICES):
THE SOUTH, LONDON AND THE NORTH, 1971-2013

Source: Martin et al. (2015)

research that uses the concept of financialisation to explore the growing power of
finance more generally (Krippner, 2005).

FINANCIALISATION: MAKING THE CONNECTIONS BETWEEN FINANCE AND THE 'REAL ECONOMY'

It is widely agreed among a range of economic commentators and social scientists
that financial logics play an increasingly important role in the economic, social and
cultural life of many, if not most, economies, particularly in Europe and North
America. The term financialisation has been developed to capture this and can be
understood, at its broadest, as signalling the growing dominance of finance and
financial services within any given economy. However, despite this agreement, using
data to specify the nature of the rise of finance, the process of financialisation and
the implications of this have proved to be more challenging. One of the earliest and
fullest such exercises was carried out by the historical sociologist Greta Krippner,
who used a number of different measures to examine the extent to which, and in
what ways, the US economy could be said to have been financialised (Krippner,
2005). These include the share of employment made up by the finance, insurance

FIGURE 4.2 RELATIVE INDUSTRY SHARES OF CORPORATE PROFITS IN US ECONOMY, 1950-2001

Source: Krippner (2005). Reprinted with permission from Oxford University Press. Permission conveyed through Copyright Clearance Centre, Inc.

and real estate (FIRE) sectors, as well as the different shares of profit from these sectors within the UK economy as shown in Figure 4.2.

However, the range of different ways in which financialisation can be measured has given rise to a number of different approaches, all within the rubric of financialisation, leading some commentators to urge caution in using the term at all:

> [W]e might ask, where does financialization in its various manifestations sit on the spectrum between powerful and innovative theory at one extreme and superficial and redundant label at the other? (Christophers, 2015: 187)

One prominent strand of this critique centres on the limited spatial imagination that has typified much of the research on financialisation (French et al., 2011). In particular, this critique argues that much of the research on financialisation has tended to see national economies as 'containers' within which financial and economic life unfold. As a result, while the changing nature of national economies and their reliance on financial services has been identified, a number of important issues and dimensions within financialisation remain comparatively neglected. This includes the ways in which corporate experiences of financial logics can be experienced differently in different regions, even within the same firm. Similarly, within any national economy, there are a myriad of ways in which individuals can experience the financial services sector, from working as a financial elite supporting the very process of financialisation itself to being marginalised and excluded from financial services, unable to obtain basic financial services such as a bank account. Moreover, these experiences are typically regionally segregated such that financial elites work and live in the more financially connected areas while those excluded from the international financial system are prevalent in less prosperous, peripheral regions.

In response, economic geographers in particular have sought to advance understandings of financialisation by examining the spatialities at work in much more detail. For example, work has identified at least three important ways in which a greater attention to the spatialities of financialisation can be instructive in better understanding the nature of the changes the term itself seeks to examine (French et al., 2011). First, there is scope to examine in more detail the variegated political causes and implications of financialisation processes. Second, greater attention needs to be paid to the intersection between the international financial system and domestic models and practices associated with money and finance, since it is precisely through this intersection that firms, individuals and households find themselves increasingly tied into the international financial system. Third, and following on, work needs to examine how financialisation not only shapes economic landscapes, but is also a product of such spaces and places as it enrols different places and activities in different ways.

In response to these critiques, a growing body of research has developed that examines how financial (il)logics are increasingly shaping the activities of households and firms such that the economic and financial futures of individuals are increasingly tied into the international financial system. In this work, financialisation is understood as 'a pattern of accumulation in which profit-making occurs increasingly through financial channels rather than through trade and commodity production' (Aalbers, 2009b: 148). Particular attention within this approach has been paid to the transformation of domestic mortgage markets from ones that were predominately aimed at acting as a 'facilitating market' that provided the credit required by households to purchase their own home, to one increasingly dominated by the logics of global investment in which mortgages as financial products are increasingly viewed by global financial institutions as having the potential to act as a revenue stream in and of themselves. In order for this to happen, mortgages are securitised and the resulting residential mortgage-backed securities (RMBS) are traded within IFCs. Securitisation is a set of financial practices, the importance of which has come to the fore following the financial crisis. It can be understood as a

> practice of 'bundling' together a stream of future obligations arising from mortgage repayments to provide the basis for the issue of, and the payment of, principal and interest on securities. (Langley, 2006: 283)

Crucially, the value of RMBS is determined by the presumed credit risk (put simply, the likelihood of default by the borrower) (see Box 4.1). As a result, households are increasingly scored based on their risk profile, and it is in this way that they find themselves tied more closely into the international financial system. Moreover, an individual's credit score becomes increasingly important in determining whether or not they can access credit, and the terms of that credit, particularly in relation to mortgages. The significance of this work is two-fold. First, its focus on the rise of credit scoring as a financial technology within financialisation has important implications in terms of households and individuals being excluded from the financial system (as explored in Chapter 7 through work on financial exclusion). Second, RMBS were central to the causes of the 2007–2008 financial crisis because it was the implementation of less stringent lending criteria to higher-risk borrowers and their subsequent default that were central to causing the crisis, beginning in so-called sub-prime (that is, higher-risk) neighbourhoods in the USA.

▬BOX 4.1▬

SECURITISATION AND THE CREATION OF RESIDENTIAL MORTGAGE-BACKED SECURITIES (RMBS)

1   The mortgage lender, the originator, produces mortgage assets and collects monthly repayments.

2   The revenue streams from mortgage assets are re-engineered based on credit risks as shown in the diagram below, showing the waterfall structure within securitisation (from Wainwright, 2009).

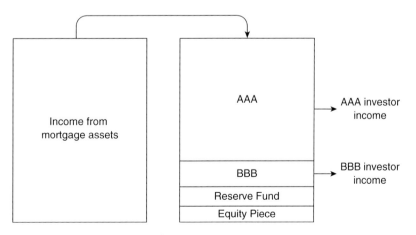

3   The lender sells these assets to a special purpose vehicle.

4   Investors including pension funds, insurance funds and hedge funds consume the securitised products.

By focusing on the relations between households and the international financial system produced through mortgage finance, this work is also important because, implicitly at least, it begins to develop a more networked approach to understanding financial systems. In this respect, a rich theoretical literature exists that can be drawn on to develop understandings of the practice, process and outcomes of financialisation.

USING NETWORKS TO UNDERSTAND THE RELATIONS BETWEEN FINANCE AND THE 'REAL ECONOMY'

Although cultural economy research has tended to understand finance as a separate realm from the 'real economy', there is a more long-standing commitment, particularly within political economy approaches to money and finance, to understand the relationship between finance and economy more generally. Indeed, some scholars have raised concerns that research attention has increasingly moved beyond this focus, and accounts of money and finance have become relatively isolated from wider accounts of the political economies of change and dynamism in the global economy (Engelen and Faulconbridge, 2009; Pike and Pollard, 2010). One of the reasons for this sense of missed opportunity in terms of studying the relationship between finance and the real economy is that, before the finance-led boom in the global economy of the 2000s, there was a much longer political economy tradition of examining the relationship between finance and broader economic processes and practices (see for example Froud et al., 2000).

Most notably, political economy approaches have been developed that build on Marx's work on the central role of money within production and exchange relationships. In terms of money and finance and its global reach, this work has been developed most fully by the geographer David Harvey, notably through his seminal book, *The Limits to Capital* (1982). This work demonstrates how money is central to a particular mode of organising the economy that is termed the capitalist mode of production. Within this system, money is put to work in the system of production, for example through investing in new machinery for a factory production line in order to realise more money than was initially put into the system. This process is captured through the term 'M-C-M' (money-commodities-money) and is based upon the means of production being held privately by individuals who are motivated to participate in the production system in order to increase their own monetary holdings and associated relative power within the economy. In so doing, in this framework, money acts as both a medium of exchange and a measure of exchange value, and it is through these functions that money becomes tied into closer networks with the economy and its production processes more generally. In terms of being a medium of exchange, money facilitates the production process. As such, money also acts as a measure of exchange value because it acts as what is known as the general equivalent. In this sense, it puts a price on different elements within the productive process such that very different types of objects can have their (monetary) value compared.

This includes both the cost of labour power involved in the production process and the cost of machinery used in production. Moreover, wealth is measured through the accumulation of money rather than through the accumulation of other forms of value such as productive equipment (Leyshon and Thrift, 1997).

Importantly, this approach draws attention to the inherently crisis-prone nature of the economy such that the owners of capital remain constantly in search of additional avenues to increase their own holdings of money. Indeed, Harvey has used this approach to explain how these crises of accumulation have been central in causing the 2007–2008 financial crisis (Harvey, 2010; 2014). For Harvey, the crisis started in the sub-prime mortgage markets, largely concentrated in the American South, which had developed essentially into debt bubbles as capital's search for ever new sources of profit led to overinflated property prices. Major financial institutions that had exposure to these markets, notably investment banks such as Bear Stearns, then acted as conduits through which the crisis was transmitted beyond North America and Western Europe (where housing market overinflation had also taken place, particularly in countries such as Spain and Ireland). This process was exacerbated by the collapse of the investment bank Lehman Brothers in 2008 because of the reputational damage that the downfall of what had been seen as an established investment bank caused to the international financial system and the credit system in particular. As a result, the global market for lending dried up and corporations and householders faced a sharp tightening up of credit lending policies. The ensuing period has been marked by a range of different state interventions aimed at stimulating economic recovery. In the USA, and initially in the UK at least, this was marked by a Keynesian-inspired approach to state support and investment in sectors such as infrastructure. However, more recently, the political landscape of North America and Western Europe has been dominated by austerity politics as the political right has sought to reframe the crisis, not as one of banking and financial services, but as one of bloated state expenditure and associated public finance debt that need to be reduced drastically in order to facilitate economic growth (Langley, 2014).

In addition to providing powerful analyses of the financial crisis, this approach to understanding the global economy has been central in stimulating interest in money and finance beyond mainstream economics and within the social sciences from the 1990s onwards. However, during the finance-led boom of the 2000s, research increasingly began to focus on finance in and of itself rather than the links between finance and the broader economy as suggested by earlier political economy research on money and finance. In the wake of the crisis, as researchers have sought to develop more politically attuned and critical understandings of the global economy, this has changed and researchers are increasingly beginning to (re)turn to political economy approaches in order to advance understandings of the relations between money, finance and the economy. For example, research has drawn on Harvey (1990) to argue that tracing financial and monetary networks could provide a useful way of defetishising money in order to pay greater attention to the wider work that money and finance do in the economy (Christophers, 2011b; 2011c).

In so doing, this approach echoes the broader social science literature that has sought to develop network understandings of the global economy, or to understand the messy relationships between money and the 'ordinary economy' (Lee, 2006).

NETWORKS AND RELATIONAL APPROACHES TO THE GLOBAL ECONOMY

Echoing these calls for a more networked understanding of money and finance, there has been a growing recognition across the social sciences that using a network approach to economic life is instructive in revealing how economic and, in the case of this book, financial networks intersect with particular locations in which they become grounded (Coe et al., 2014; Dicken et al., 2001; Pollard and Samers, 2007; 2013). This emphasis on the intersection between flows, of finance in the case of this chapter, and the territorial bases of economies follows wider work that is commonly labelled the 'mobility turn' within the social sciences that not only emphasises questions of mobility, but is also concerned with 'how all mobilities entail specific, often highly embedded and immobile infrastructures' (Sheller and Urry, 2006: 210). Network approaches to studying the economy, as applied to financial services, are particularly useful in developing cultural economy approaches to money and finance because both literatures are influenced by actor network theory and therefore emphasise the range of agents involved in the production and maintenance of economic networks. Indeed, research has gone as far as to argue that the network literature provides a 'methodology for analysing the global economy' (Dicken et al., 2001: 91).

One of the ways in which these insights have been developed most comprehensively in the social sciences is through research on global production networks which forms part of a wider programme of work that seeks to explain 'how global industries are organized and governed, and how, in turn, those relationships affect the development and upgrading opportunities of the various regions and firms' (Coe et al., 2008: 267). In particular, by combining global production chains approaches with wider cultural-economy-style research into actor network theory, as well as an appreciation of the variegated nature of national business systems, this work 'aims to reveal the multi-actor and multi-scalar characteristics of transnational production systems through intersecting notions of power, value and embeddedness' (Coe et al., 2008: 267). While this agenda has been developed most fully through research into large multinational firms operating in sectors such as retail (Coe and Wrigley, 2007), more recent attention has focused on the links between these networks and the international financial system. This work has focused on demonstrating the close links between global production and global financial networks and the important, but comparatively neglected, role that finance plays in shaping corporate activity and its co-constitutive relationship with regional economies (Coe et al., 2014). In so doing it brings together an appreciation of the range of different spaces involved in the international financial system, including both on- and offshore financial centres (discussed in Chapter 5), and the key role played by advanced producer services,

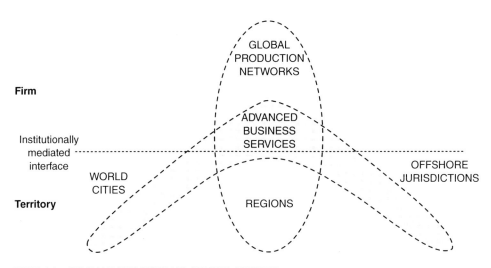

FIGURE 4.3 THE GLOBAL PRODUCTION AND FINANCIAL NETWORKS

Source: Coe et al. (2014)

including finance, law firms and management consultancy, in articulating these links (Wójcik, 2013). This relationship is illustrated in Figure 4.3.

As this figure shows, work on global financial networks specifies the relationship between finance and the rest of the economy, in the form of global production networks, by taking advanced producer services at its starting point since these firms are central in producing, selling and developing the financial products that form the link between finance and the real economy. The geography of these firms is concentrated in a small number of world cities although, as we shall see in Chapter 5, they make significant use of offshore jurisdictions through their financial activity. In so doing, they provide the link between the globally connected, yet regionally manifested, process of economic development through global production networks, linking these regional geographies to the activities of world cities, international financial centres and the offshore world.

Beyond specific work that builds on the tradition of global production networks (GPNs), research has taken financial networks as its starting point, rather than inserting finance into other types of networks, as characterises the GPN literature. This approach argues that although the firm is often placed at the heart of economic analysis, critical social science understanding of firm finance remains comparatively limited. This can be attributed to wider approaches within economies. First, in neo-classical economics, finance is identified as a factor of production, the spatiality of which is not important; and, second, with some exceptions the history of political economy thought has emphasised the 'real' economy rather than demonstrating a strong interest in the ways in which firm finance intersects with the 'real economy' (Pollard, 2003). More recently, networked geographical imaginations are increasingly being used to examine the intersections between finance and the 'real economy'. This work places financial networks at the heart of its analysis and argues that research needs to explore 'the inescapable geographic construction, context and rootedness of financial networks and practices' (Pike and Pollard, 2010: 38). Such an approach demands a more relational and networked understanding of finance because 'financial', from this perspective, is understood as a cross-scalar network, ranging from individuals, through firms and sectors, to regional and national economies, some of which are more territorially fixed while others act as pipelines between these territorial economies.

This approach has been deployed in a number of different types of financial services. For example, work on Islamic finance has used this approach to move beyond a straightforward binary between Islamic and 'western' finance to demonstrate the ways in which these financial systems often co-exist in IFCs and intersect with each other in complex ways (Pollard and Samers, 2007; 2013; see also Chapter 3). In terms of retail finance, work has examined how retail bank branch networks in the USA and UK have facilitated the 'circulation of conventions of restructuring' (Leyshon and Pollard, 2000: 204) such that the practices of US and UK retail banks have converged, in part through changes in the regulatory landscape of the two markets. Finally, an extensive literature has developed that explores how alternative financial networks intersect with the communities in which they are (re)produced (Leyshon et al., 2003).

There are three significant advantages of developing these more networked and relational understandings of the relationship between financial networks and economic practices more generally. First, by tracing financial networks, a number of new actors and processes can be identified through which economies are constituted at the intersection of finance and wider economic practices. Second, a focus on the (re)production of networks between finance and the rest of the economy responds to calls for a more critically and politically engaged cultural economy approach to money and finance, by examining the power both in and of networks. In this sense, a focus on networks reveals the importance of power relations within networks as these networks are planned, developed and maintained. However, they can also be thought of as achieving structural power within an economy (Dicken et al., 2001). Third, a focus on networks takes seriously the time–space specificity of financial and economic relations, documenting their variegated nature and thereby moving beyond the methodological nationalism that has typified much of the research on financialisation to date.

FIRM AND FINANCIAL NETWORKS

Given the centrality of firm finances within the financialisation literature, in many ways it is not surprising that one of the main areas of focus for work on the networked relationship between financial and wider economic networks has been on firm finances and the different ways in which firms intersect with the international financial system. Indeed, 'financial narratives' (O'Neill, 2001) have become increasingly powerful within firms operating in a range of sectors, from manufacturing to advanced professional services such as law firms (see respectively Faulconbridge and Muzio, 2009; Froud et al., 2002). While this has also been a central concern within the financialisation literature, a focus on firm-finance networks has allowed the spatialities both constituted by and shaped by such relations to be more fully understood. This approach builds on wider commitments to revealing the ways in which firms are embedded within particular territorial economies, as well as choreographing a range of different flows (of people, capital and goods, for example) between these economies (Dicken and Malmberg, 2001).

A number of different case study firms have been examined within this approach. For example, in the case of engineering and aerospace, research has used a networked reading of financialisation to understand the relocation of Boeing's corporate headquarters to Chicago from Puget Sound on the west coast of the USA (Muellerleile, 2009). The initial headquarter location of Puget Sound reflected the company's embedding within the engineering culture above financial imperatives. The move to Chicago has therefore been interpreted as demonstrating a desire within the firm to improve its access to financial services at favourable rates, with this being achieved, at least in part, by moving to a financial centre in the shape of Chicago, thereby marking a break with the engineering culture that was seen to dominate in Puget Sound. In other cases, research has demonstrated how the financial services produced in leading financial centres such as London intersect with firm practices beyond IFCs in regional economies and provincial cities. In the case of North America and Western Europe, the growing importance attached to financial governance of firms, exemplified by the growing influence of chief financial officers vis-à-vis chief executive officers, has given rise to the growing prioritisation of financial returns, often with significant implications for the regional economies in which firms are located beyond the most successful financial regions.

In the case of the UK, this is particularly the case in terms of firms operating in more economically depressed regions. Particular research attention has been paid to the north east of England in this respect, reflecting its growth as a manufacturing region but one that has, following the financial crisis, suffered significant cuts in public spending expenditure which became an essential part of the region's economy following processes of deindustrialisation from the 1980s onwards. In this respect, research has examined the closure of socially and economically significant firms including the Vaux Brewery (see Figure 4.4) in the city of Sunderland (Pike, 2006). Initially a specialist brewing company, it subsequently expanded into the hotel business. As part of this refocusing, the company was advised by a subsidiary of the investment bank Deutsche Bank to sell the brewing business, although it remained profitable. This sale was agreed in 1999 and seen as a victory for financial logics produced in financial centres, particularly London, above the long-standing commitment to brewing in the north East of England that the company had produced. Indeed, the sell-off resulted in the resignation of the Chairman, Sir Paul Nicholson. Further work on the north east of England has demonstrated the ways in which the region was hit by the financial crisis, not least through the demise

	Main company	Acquisitions and mergers	Disposals and *closures*
1837	C. Vaux		
1871		Founding of Castle Brewery (Sunderland)	
1919		Lorimer & Clark's Caledonian Brewery (Edinburgh)[a]	
1927	Associated Breweries Ltd	North Eastern Breweries plc	
1934		Berwick Breweries[b]	
1937		Ridley, Cutter and Firth (Newcastle)	
1943	Name changed to Vaux and Associated Breweries Ltd		
1947		Hepworth & Co. (Ripon) Whitwell, Mark & Co. (Kendal)	
1954		Steel, Coulson & Co. (Edinburgh)	
1959		Thomas Usher & Son (Edinburgh)	
1961		John Wright & Co. (Perth)	
1964			*John Wright & Co. (Perth)*
1972		S.H. Ward & Co. (Sheffield)	
1973	Vaux Breweries Ltd[c]		
1974		Liefmans (Belgium)	
1978		W.M. Darley Ltd (Thorne)	
1979			Lorimers Brewery (formerly Thomas Usher & Son) following disposal to Allied Breweries
1980		Trident (Tyne Tees TV) (20%)	
1981[d]		Fred Koch Brewery (New York State, USA)	
1984			Fred Koch Brewery (New York State, USA)
1985	Vaux Group plc		
1986			Caledonian MBO Brewery (management buy out) (Edinburgh) M. W. M. Darley Ltd (Thorne) Liefmans (Belgium)
1987[e]			
1990			Wines & Spirits Division to Greenalls (now de Vere) Trident (Tyne Tees TV) Care Homes Division
1999	Swallow Group plc		
1999	Acquisition by Whitbread[f]		

[a]Sir Paul Nicholson's grandfather's independent purchase.
[b]Brewery closed and site retained as bottling plant.
[c]Swallow Hotels Division established.
[d]Off-license division (Blayney & Co.) established.
[e]Care home division (St. Andrew's Homes Ltd) established.
[f]Whtbread acquired IS breweries between 1960 and 1990.

FIGURE 4.4   CORPORATE EVOLUTION OF THE VAUX BREWERY, 1837-1999

Source: Pike (2006). Reprinted with permission from Oxford University Press. Permission conveyed through Copyright Clearance Centre, Inc.

of the local building society, Northern Rock, which had been headquartered in Newcastle (Marshall et al., 2011). In so doing, this work demonstrates how the intersection between firm and financial networks needs to be appreciated in order to understand and explain the nature of uneven economic development at the regional level. This has been largely overlooked by much of the financialisation literature and also echoes the development of work on GPNs and global financial networks discussed above.

INFRASTRUCTURE AND FINANCIAL NETWORKS

The intersection between financial circuits and the broader economy has also been examined through a network approach through work that focuses on the role of financial networks in shaping the built and increasingly the natural environments via processes of financialisation that have been labelled the 'capitalization of almost everything' (Leyshon and Thrift, 2007). By focusing on infrastructure in particular, such as public utilities of water, electricity and power networks, this work provides a useful corrective focus to the seemingly glamorous elements of 'high finance' within IFCs (Leyshon and Thrift, 2007). However, this world of finance relies on finding new 'fixed assets that will yield a predictable income stream' (Leyshon and Thrift, 2007: 99) that often stem from the taken-for-granted, far less glamorous elements of everyday life.

Work in this area has been concerned with the relationship between infrastructure provision, particularly in cities, and financial networks. In part, this interest in infrastructure has been triggered by the 2007–2008 financial crisis as several Western European and North American states have increasingly seen infrastructure as an important potential vehicle in stimulating economic recovery. This is particularly true in countries in which austerity politics have resulted in significant declines in state funding, as alternative financial forms of provision to fund infrastructure development then become an increasingly attractive option for managing to balance the dual requirements of stimulating economic recovery and reducing public sector spending (O'Brien and Pike, 2015). This work seeks to understand both the funding of infrastructure associated with how its users pay for its use (as in the case of road tolls, for example) and the financing of infrastructure that 'involves the costs incurred by actors in the provision of capital both in terms of the services of putting together the financing arrangements and the actual cost of capital' (O'Brien and Pike, 2015: R15).

For example, the water network in the UK has been the subject of a process of financialisation since it was privatised in 1989 as part of the widespread privatisation agenda followed by Prime Minister Margaret Thatcher. The names of the former regional water authorities (such as Severn, Anglian and Welsh Water) have remained. However, the changing nature of ownership behind these names reveals the ways in which the delivery of everyday household water in the UK is increasingly tied into the activities and fortunes of the international financial system. Initially, these water companies were purchased by large, often multinational energy firms such as Veolia. However, over time, they have been increasingly purchased by specialist

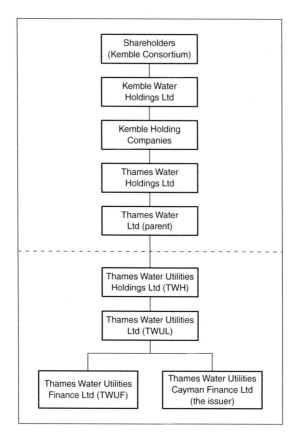

FIGURE 4.5   CORPORATE STRUCTURE OF THAMES WATER UTILITIES GROUP

Source: Standard & Poor's, 'Thames Water Utilities Cayman Finance Ltd.', *Global Credit Portal* (2008) p. 4.

infrastructure investment funds seeking to securitise the revenue streams that stem from household water bills:

> In the hands of financial intermediaries … a guaranteed revenue stream over time can be securitised, that is, turned into a tradable financial product, broken up into separate earnings packages, assigned a risk profile and sold onto investors seeking long-term real returns. (Allen and Pryke, 2013: 422)

For example, the consortium of shareholders (Kemble Consortium) behind Thames Water is owned by Kemble Water Holdings Limited, which in turn is owned by a number of pension and infrastructure funds as shown in Figure 4.5. One of the consequences of such a networked ownership structure is that the political implications of such a financialised business model have remained relatively hidden, even from the water regulator in the UK, which raises important questions about the nature of infrastructure delivery when financial demands and claims on income streams dominate organisational logics.

CONCLUSIONS

This chapter has sought to combine cultural economy research with political economy approaches to money and finance in order to position finance more clearly within wider economic relations. In particular, the analysis has drawn on the growing interest in networks and relations, particularly the power relations associated with these. Such an approach is important because it responds to calls to develop a more politically and critically attuned understanding of the international financial system, particularly in the wake of the 2007–2008 financial crisis, thereby addressing some of the perceived limitations of cultural economy research on money and finance (Hall, 2011). The work discussed in this chapter achieves this by moving away from understanding finance in and of itself and therefore potentially glamorising it, to reveal the important role of finance in shaping more mundane economic activities and in so doing reshaping political economies in several economies in Western Europe and North America. As the chapter demonstrates, the implications of such an approach are wide ranging, addressing some of the central issues surrounding the operation of contemporary finance-led capitalism. They include: questions of access to finance and credit in particular for individuals; patterns of uneven regional development; and the infrastructure provision we rely on in our everyday lives.

KEY FURTHER READINGS

Krippner, G. (2005) The financialization of the American economy. *Socio-Economic Review*, 3: 173–208.
This is one of the foundational texts that seeks to present empirical data at the national level in the USA to support claims that the US economy has become financialised.

Leyshon, A. and Thrift, N. (2007) The capitalization of almost everything: the future of finance and capitalism. *Theory, Culture and Society*, 24: 97–115.
This paper examines the myriad connections that have developed between finance and the rest of the economy in recent years.

Pike, A. (2006) 'Shareholder value' versus the regions: the closure of the Vaux Brewery in Sunderland. *Journal of Economic Geography*, 6: 201–222.
This paper presents a detailed examination of the relationship between shareholder value and regional economic development through a case study of the north east of England.

5

FINANCE, PRODUCTION AND THE RISE OF NEW OFFSHORE SPACES

- Introduction
- Identifying offshore financial centres
  - *Island economies as OFCs*
  - *The rise of new types of OFCs?*
- Blurring the boundary between on- and offshore financial space
  - *On- and offshore financial networks beyond Europe and North America*
  - *Private wealth and the rise of midshore financial centres*
  - *The case of Singapore and Hong Kong as midshore financial centres*
- Conclusions

INTRODUCTION

One of the most widely reported financial stories in the wake of the financial crisis has been the payment of tax, or lack of it, by multinational corporations. For example, in the UK attention has focused on firms from a range of sectors that are household names, including McDonald's, Google, Starbucks and Apple, based around data that showed the comparatively low level of tax paid compared with the revenue of these companies (*Guardian*, 2012) (see Figure 5.1). This was set against the wider backdrop of a number of well-known UK companies being taken over by their US rivals. These corporate restructurings ushered in a period of concern surrounding the implications of these takeovers for UK jobs and the regional and city economies in which they were embedded. Most notably, in 2010, the US food multinational Kraft took over the UK chocolate company Cadbury. However, such

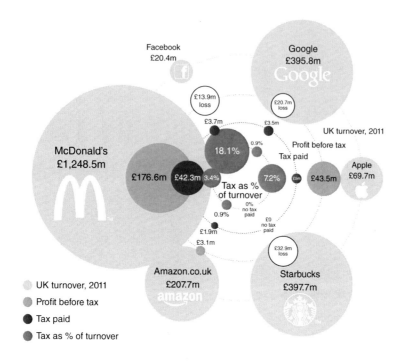

Facebook
£20.4m

Google
£395.8m

£13.9m
loss

£20.7m
loss

£3.7m   £3.5m

UK turnover, 2011

McDonald's
£1,248.5m

18.1%   0.9%   Profit before tax
Tax paid

£176.6m £42.3m 3.4%   7.2% £5m £43.5m   Apple
£69.7m

Tax as %
of turnover

0%
no tax
0.9%   paid

£0
no tax
£1.9m   paid

£3.1m

£32.9m
loss

UK turnover, 2011
Profit before tax
Tax paid
Tax as % of turnover

Amazon.co.uk
£207.7m

Starbucks
£397.7m

FIGURE 5.1   TAX PAID BY MAJOR US COMPANIES IN THE UK

Source: Guardian (2012). Image and data credit © DueDil Ltd. Reprinted with permission.

was the concern over this deal that the Panel of Takeovers and Mergers reviewed the Takeover Code and made changes in September 2011 with the aim of giving the target firm more power in the negotiations, particularly in terms of a better understanding of the intentions of the buyer post-takeover. Nevertheless, this has been followed by other notable takeovers such as the acquisition of the leading high street pharmacy and beauty company in the UK, Boots, by the American firm Walgreens. Meanwhile, beyond a focus on the tax affairs of large corporations, considerable political and popular attention was focused on how the most wealthy individuals globally have maintained and developed their wealth through the use of offshore places and practices, as in the leaking of the so-called 'Panama Papers' in April 2016. These documents from the Panamanian firm Mossack Fonseca reveal the ways in which private wealth is reproduced through a range of offshore centres and activities.

These developments raise two important questions concerning the ability of existing cultural economy approaches to money and finance to be able to understand and explain these elements of firm finances – questions that form the focus of this chapter. First, the growing interest in tax evasion demonstrates that accounts of global finance need to move beyond the financial heartlands of global finance – namely, IFCs. While cultural economy research has focused on these financial centres, particularly in North America and Europe, the case of corporate tax evasion suggests that more elaborate financial networks cross-cutting different jurisdictions also need to be traced to understand how firm finances are managed through a combination of both on- and offshore financial centres.

This chapter addresses this issue by developing work on offshore finance that emerged from the 1990s onwards within a range of social science disciplines including economic geography, international relations and economic sociology. This work provides a helpful starting point in understanding the function and form of offshore financial centres (OFCs). However, as will be shown, the places that can be classified as OFCs have changed in recent years. This raises important questions concerning the ability of earlier work on OFCs to account for and understand more recent changes in the nature of offshore finance and its relationship with more well-established IFCs. In response, this chapter examines these new offshore financial spaces and the ways in which they trouble a neat separation between on- and offshore financial space. In so doing, the chapter also examines the rise of what have become known as midshore financial centres (such as Singapore and Hong Kong) that combine elements of both on- and offshore financial space.

Second, as noted above, the continued importance of offshore financial spaces and centres also draws attention to the ways in which financial networks not only comprise corporate wealth, but also involve the growing importance of private wealth held by the most wealthy in society globally. The role of private wealth has not been as widely studied in work on offshore finance when compared with the use of offshore space by firms and corporations (Beaverstock et al., 2013a). To a significant extent, this reflects the ways in which obtaining data on private wealth, by definition, is very difficult. Indeed, the most readily available such sources come from international consultancy firms that are tasked with supporting the private wealth management industry that has developed to provide bespoke financial services to these very wealthy individuals (Beaverstock et al., 2013b). As a result of their close relationship with the industry, these reports are often rather promotional in tone, rather than engaging critically with the development of the private wealth management industry. However, while care needs to be taken in interpreting the findings of these reports, they do agree on a marked increase in the number of wealthy people globally and an associated increase in the volume of private wealth available to invest. For example, in 1996 Capgemini Merrily Lynch (CML) (2007) estimated that 4.5 million high-net-worth individuals (defined as individuals with investable assets of over $1 million) were present globally with a collective wealth of US$16.6 trillion. By 2010, this number had increased to 10.9 million with an associated wealth of US$42.7 trillion (Beaverstock et al., 2013b).

In response to these developments, this chapter examines both corporate and private wealth uses of offshore financial space and the consequences of this for the nature of offshore financial space itself, the services it offers and the networks that are created between on- and offshore jurisdictions. In so doing, it develops cultural economy research that has identified the importance of particular financial technologies or 'market devices' (Muniesa et al., 2007) in the construction of financial markets. However, to date, this approach has not been widely employed in the study of offshore finance. The analysis in this chapter suggests that bringing the cultural economy literature into closer dialogue with understandings of offshore finance provides a valuable way of enhancing the conceptual toolkit of cultural economy research and networked understandings of money and finance, as well as providing valuable empirical and conceptual insights into the changing nature of offshore financial space and centres in particular.

IDENTIFYING OFFSHORE FINANCIAL CENTRES

A central issue that needs to be addressed in the study of OFCs is a definitional one concerning both the spaces that can be defined as offshore and the financial and related business service activities (such as legal and tax advice) that take place within them. The term offshore itself is problematic since it conjures up images of islands that are literally offshore and remote from mainland IFCs. As we shall see, although these islands are part of the offshore financial world, they are not the only spaces that constitute offshore finance. However, in order to be more precise about what we mean by offshore finance, it is instructive to consider both the types of financial services activity that take place offshore and the geographical locations in which these activities take place. Beginning with the financial functions of offshore space, the IMF defines offshore finance as

> at its simplest, the provision of financial services by banks and other agents to non-residents. These services include the borrowing of money from non-residents and lending to non-residents. This can take the form of lending to corporates and other financial institutions, funded by liabilities to offices of the lending bank elsewhere, or to market participants. (See www.imf.org/external/np/mae/oshore/2000/eng/back.htm#II)

This definition is important because it signals that the nature of offshore finance relies on offering financial services in any given place to non-residents of that location. As such, what are often conceived of as onshore financial centres such as London could potentially fall into this category, given their important role in offering financial services to non-UK-domiciled, very wealthy elites through the wealth management industry, a development explored later in the chapter. The IMF goes on to specify that offshore financial spaces contain financial assets and liabilities that are far larger and consequently out of proportion with those needed to provide financial intermediation services to their domestic economic activity. Finally, OFCs typically offer clients low or even zero taxation, comparatively lower levels of regulation as compared with their onshore counterparts, and a high degree of secrecy and anonymity in their financial and taxation affairs.

However, the IMF definition does not say very much about the use of OFCs in relation to private as opposed to corporate wealth. Moreover, it does not specify the different types of places that could and do act as OFCs. In this respect, one of the earliest and most useful sets of definitions of offshore financial spaces is provided in a four-fold typology of different types of OFCs (Park, 1982). First, reflecting the possibility that offshore financial services could be offered within IFCs, this work identifies primary OFCs. These are full-service banking and financial services that lie at the heart of the international system, including London and New York. Second, booking centres are offshore centres that offer only banking services, rather than capital market services. These centres are important for what are termed 'shell companies' where economic activities are booked in order to avoid taxation, something we examine in more detail later on in the chapter. Third, funding centres act as conduits that enable the movement of offshore funds into the local and regional markets, including places such as Panama. Finally, collection centres offer intermediation services to wider OFCs, such as Bahrain.

ISLAND ECONOMIES AS OFCs

In terms of the development of these different approaches to offshore finance, most early research from the late 1990s onwards focused on the importance of small (geographically) island economies within the international system (Hampton and Christensen, 1999; Warf, 2002) (see Table 5.1). Particular research attention has been paid to the case of the Caribbean, notably the Cayman Islands and Bahamas, within this literature as this region provided an important range of offshore financial services for leading financial centres in North America, particularly the USA and Western Europe (Cobb, 1998; 1999; Hudson, 1998; 2000; Roberts, 1994; 1995). The role of these Caribbean islands as OFCs can be dated back to the 1960s although they were already classified as tax havens at that point (Shaxson, 2012). For these small island economies, with limited natural resources and small domestic economies, developing their financial services activities through becoming an OFC was an attractive developmental strategy following independence from Jamaica in the case of the Cayman Islands, and the UK in the case of the Bahamas.

In addition to these supply-side factors in their development of OFCs, increased financial regulation in the USA created the demand for locations with comparatively lower levels of regulation that would be more attractive places for undertaking financial services transactions. In part, these regulatory developments in the USA were an important component in the development of Eurodollar markets in London (Hudson, 1998) – an early example of how what is typically understood as an onshore IFC can also house offshore financial activities (see also Chapter 1). At one level then, the development of the Bahamas and Cayman Islands follows a networked reading of global finance in which their relationship with large onshore markets was a significant element in their initial development as OFCs. In particular, their relatively low levels of regulation compared with large onshore markets, notably the USA, were very

TABLE 5.1   INDICATIVE DATA FOR SELECTED ISLAND OFFSHORE FINANCIAL CENTRES (OFCs), 2000

OFC	Offshore banks	Number employed in OFC	Assets (A) or liabilities (L) US$ (bn)	Offshore companies	Captive insurance companies
Bahrain[a]	37	NA	85.7 A	NA	NA
British Virgin Islands[a]	9	NA	NA	400,000	190
Cayman Islands	464	2,100 (1996)	648 A (1998)	59,922	522 (2001)
Cyprus	30	2,140 (1996)	8.5 L (1999)	24,000 (1996)	9 (1993)
Guernsey	77	5,000	95.7 L	15,453 (1999)	369 (2001)
Jersey	70	8,000	164.1 L	33,000	167 (2001)
Labuan	60	NA	19.5 A	2,721	68
Netherlands Antilles	45	NA	36.4 A	30,000 (1988)	21

Source: Hampton and Christensen (2002)

important. However, there were also elements of their own economies that were important. In this respect, trust is a particularly important element of OFCs' (re)production since clients using them have to have confidence that the privacy promised to them and the regulatory environment, particularly in terms of taxation rates, will be upheld. In this respect, the fact that both islands had previously been colonies becomes an important part of the story of their development. For the Bahamas in particular, their previous links with the UK that were maintained to some extent through its membership of the Commonwealth were used to demonstrate its legitimacy as an economic centre in which elements more associated with financial services in London such as the fostering of trust through networks of 'gentlemanly capitalism' were central (Augar, 2001; for a full discussion of trust in financial products more generally, see Clark and O'Connor, 1997).

Meanwhile, a closely related literature developed from the 1990s onwards that focused on tax havens (Palan, 1998). Although tax havens are not easily distinguishable from OFCs, the focus on this literature is more on a continuum of practices that render a place a tax haven, ranging from zero or at least extremely low levels of tax to places that charge tax but maintain a high degree of secrecy provision, leading to episodes of tax avoidance and money laundering (see Hampton and Abbot, 1999; Hampton and Christensen, 2002; Maurer, 2008; Shaxson, 2012; Sikka, 2003; Sikka and Willmott, 2010). Taking low rates of tax first, this work demonstrates how places which are often assumed to be tax havens, such as Jersey, Guernsey and Switzerland, typically make a distinction between resident and non-resident taxpayers such that local residents cannot use, or in the case of Jersey are penalised for using, the location's tax haven status. That said, those using the various tax avoidance schemes generally pay a charge at the opening of their fund or account. These tax havens are typically located in close proximity to, and receive support from, major onshore economic and financial centres, as typifies the relationship between the Channel Islands and the Isle of Man with the UK. The second way of operating as a tax haven is to focus on banking secrecy laws. In centres such as the Bahamas and Cayman Islands, this is achieved through legislation that makes it illegal to reveal any banking information – what is known as intentional negligence – such that limited due diligence is undertaken prior to the opening of a trust and the establishment of financial entities, the ownership and structure of which are very hard to track down.

Reflecting the growing issues and criticisms of offshore finance, the social science literature became increasingly critical in tone from the late 1990s onwards (Palan, 1998; 2006; Palan et al., 2010). At one level, this entailed a greater focus on practices of tax evasion within OFCs as well as examining the implications for small island economies if they focused almost exclusively on financial services as a source of growth (Shaxson and Christensen, 2013). Meanwhile, a significant amount of work has been conducted by non-governmental organisations concerned with fostering greater transparency within the international financial system. This literature seeks to demonstrate the implications for economies more generally of the growing importance of offshore financial networks (see Oxfam, 2009; Tax Justice Network, 2005). One central insight of this work has been the more pervasive nature of offshore finance within global finance such that it cannot be neatly separated from its onshore counterparts and is therefore not a geographically distant set of economic and financial practices that take place solely in small island economies. In order to document this changing nature of OFCs, it is instructive to begin by considering their geography.

THE RISE OF NEW TYPES OF OFCs?

A key characteristic of the earlier literature on OFCs discussed above is the identification of a distinctive geography to these different types of OFCs. Indeed, particular clusters of OFCs have been identified that each related to a major onshore financial centre or centres. For example, Europe has close links with the offshore centres of Cyprus, Guernsey, Jersey, Malta, the Isle of Man, Ireland, Monaco, Andorra and Switzerland. Meanwhile, a range of Caribbean islands including the Cayman Islands, the Bahamas and the British Virgin Islands have, in effect, acted as the cluster of OFCs for financial centres in the Americas. More recently, these geographies of offshore finance have been updated while maintaining a focus on their networked and relational qualities, through examining the foreign direct investment (FDI) flows between on- and offshore financial centres (Haberly and Wójcik, 2015). As Figure 5.2 demonstrates, a focus on FDI shows that the global financial system can be broken down into four interconnected mega-regions: Pax Americana, based around the Americas; one based around the historical legacies of the British Empire; one focused on the former USSR; and one based around Asia and particularly Greater China. Importantly, each of these regions contains what are typically assumed to be leading onshore financial centres such as London, as well as a range of OFCs, thereby troubling a straightforward separation between on- and offshore financial space (something that is picked up on later in this chapter).

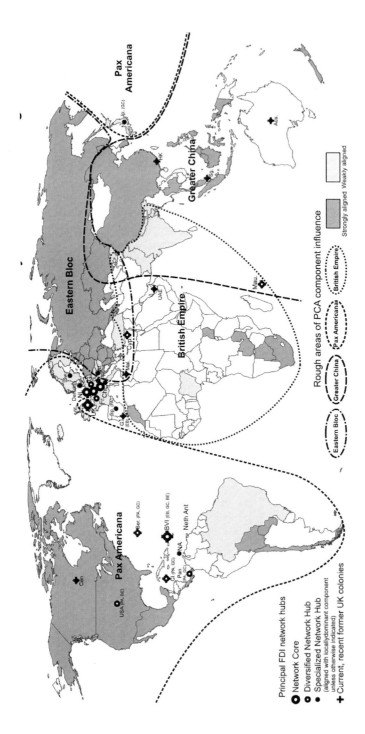

FIGURE 5.2 GLOBAL FINANCIAL REGIONS BASED ON FDI ANALYSIS

Source: 'Regional blocks and imperial legacies: mapping the global offshore FOi network', adapted from Haberly and Wojcik, *Economic Geography* 91 (3) 2015, p. 269, reprinted by permission of the publisher Taylor & Francis Ltd, http://www.tandfonline.com.

This growing recognition of the lack of a clear boundary between on- and offshore financial space has been studied as part of a wider resurrection of interest in OFCs in a number of social science disciplines in the wake of the 2007–2008 financial crisis. For example, in addition to documenting the changing nature of offshore finance through analysing FDI flows, the use of particular financial products that cross-cut on- and offshore financial space has been examined. For example, special purpose vehicles (through which assets are stored with the assistance of a range of corporate service providers, including lawyers, financiers and accountants) have created elements of offshore financial space in terms of tax avoidance within what are often seen as onshore centres such as London (Wainwright, 2011).

This work has been given an increased urgency following the financial crisis because offshore financial spaces have been shown to be important in both the causes and consequences of the crisis. For example, the term shadow banking is widely dated back to 2007 and is understood as forms of financial intermediation undertaken by regulated banks off their balance sheets (see Palan and Nesvetailova, 2014; Rixen, 2013). Recent estimates suggest that, prior to the financial crisis, the shadow banking industry was bigger than the official banking sector, and it has continued to grow with transactions taking place within offshore jurisdictions in order to keep them off the balance sheet (Bakk-Simon et al., 2012; Ghosh et al., 2012). Work on shadow banking is important because it moves the understanding of OFCs beyond an emphasis on tax evasion (on which see Palan et al., 2010; Palan and Nesvetailova, 2014) to show the diversity of financial functions that are taking place under the regulatory radar beyond tax evasion, sometimes within what are usually classified as onshore financial centres. Meanwhile, in addition to shadow banking, a number of other financial institutions that have become increasingly important actors within the post-crisis international financial system have been shown to rely on offshore financial jurisdictions, such as private equity firms and hedge funds (see Johannesen, 2014; Zucman, 2013).

More recently, there has been a growing interest in the different ways in which on- and offshore financial space are interconnected. For example, in the work on global financial networks discussed in Chapter 4, advanced producer service firms, particularly those offering legal and accountancy services, have been shown to be critical in linking on- and offshore financial space through the provision of a range of financial products that enable firms to use offshore financial space to 'manage' their tax liabilities, for example (see Seabrooke and Wigan, 2014; Wójcik, 2013).

Meanwhile, a still comparatively small but important literature has developed that identifies the importance of what are termed midshore financial centres, as a way of overcoming the distinction between on- and offshore space (see Coe et al., 2014; Sarre, 2007; Seabrooke and Wigan, 2014; Wainwright, 2011; Wójcik, 2012). Building on well-established relational perspectives within economic geography (Bathelt and Gluckler, 2003; Yeung, 2005), a central insight of this more recent work on offshore finance is the way in which it problematises a straightforward binary distinction between on- and offshore jurisdictions (see Urry, 2014). For example, this research has examined the development of offshore financial characteristics such as low levels of tax and regulation within what are typically assumed to be onshore financial spaces through the case of places such as Delaware and Miami (Maurer, 2008; Sikka, 2003). Building on this combination of offshore financial activities within onshore financial space, a growing interest can be found within the social sciences on the development of midshore financial centres that 'combine offshore advantages (low taxes, secrecy) with onshore traits (strong legal systems, double taxation treaties, sophisticated financial markets)' (see also Clark et al., 2015; Cobham et al., 2015; Coe et al., 2014: 765).

BLURRING THE BOUNDARY BETWEEN ON- AND OFFSHORE FINANCIAL SPACE

The best way of understanding this myriad of ways in which offshore space is becoming entwined with onshore financial space, leading to the development of work on midshore finance, is through an examination of particular financial activities and places. In what follows, we consider the case of a particular firm, China Mobile, before turning to the experience of particular places that are increasingly being identified as midshore financial centres.

ON- AND OFFSHORE FINANCIAL NETWORKS BEYOND EUROPE AND NORTH AMERICA

Much of the work examining offshore financial space has focused either on OFCs that service financial centres in Europe and North America or on the use of offshore financial space by firms headquartered in Europe and North America. However, as Figure 5.2 shows, on- and offshore financial relations characterise the nature of financial services more globally. In this respect the case of China Mobile is particularly instructive (Wójcik and Camilleri, 2015). China Mobile was founded in 1997 and is one of the first 'national champions' within mainland China to lead the 'going out', or internationalisation strategy, within the telecommunications sector as part of the wider internationalisation of the Chinese economy. It is also the largest telecommunications company in the world by market capitalisation. However, a seemingly straightforward interrogation of where this company is headquartered reveals its growing use of offshore financial space. For example, its annual report has it registered in Hong Kong while other financial documentation states that it has regional headquarters throughout the Chinese provinces. Meanwhile the Fortune Global 500 lists it as being headquartered in Beijing.

Research has shown that the way to solve the puzzle as to where China Mobile is located is to examine its financial affairs, and particularly its initial public offering in 1997. In this respect, the offering involved the participation of a number of advanced producer service firms, notably global investment banks led by Goldman

Sachs, leading corporate law firms and accountancy firms. Goldman Sachs acted as the coordinator for the offering and in this role would have been responsible for determining the value of the company and advising the Chinese government on the structure of the issue. Focusing on these firms reveals the dynamic relationships between different IFCs and OFCs within the offering. Although the major advanced business services (ABS) firms involved in the deal were headquartered in Europe and North America, they initially used their Hong Kong offices to help facilitate the deal, but as the transaction progressed, the importance of Hong Kong declined and Beijing became increasingly important as firms sought to be close to the key political and regulatory decision makers for the Chinese economy who are located in the city (see Chapter 3 on the changing balance of power between financial centres in Asia). Meanwhile, further research reveals that 74 per cent of China Mobile is in fact a company registered in the British Virgin Islands, a key offshore financial centre for the Chinese economy (Wójcik and Camilleri, 2015). Furthermore, Hong Kong also remains an important financial node within the company, acting in effect as a midshore financial centre between the political power held in Beijing and the company's offshore activity in the BVI. To complicate this network further, the offshore activities in the BVI remain tied to onshore financial space through their continued reliance on leading global ABS firms that are located in established IFCs.

The case of China Mobile is therefore instructive in revealing both the ways in which firm finances can cross-cut on- and offshore financial space and the ways in which different geographical networks emerge when research attention is decentred beyond firms located in IFCs in the Global North and attention is paid to firms from rapidly emerging economies, notably China.

PRIVATE WEALTH AND THE RISE OF MIDSHORE FINANCIAL CENTRES

As noted above, an important element in the changing nature of OFCs has been their role in facilitating, and being reliant upon, the rise of a private wealth management industry that provides financial services aimed at protecting, maintaining and enhancing the wealth of the richest individuals globally (Beaverstock et al., 2013a). A focus on this part of the global financial services industry is instructive in revealing the rise of what have become known as midshore financial centres that combine elements of both on- and offshore financial space. This industry also reflects the growing importance of the Asia–Pacific region within the international financial system. Indeed, figures show that, in addition to the overall increase in the most wealthy as noted above, there has been a marked change in the location of high-net-worth individuals and the associated location of their private wealth. The usual measure of these individuals, known in the industry as high-net-worth individuals (HNWIs), is that they have investable assets of greater than $1 million. Historically, North America and Europe have typically accounted for at least two-thirds of both the number of HNWIs globally and the volume of private wealth held

TABLE 5.2   THE DISTRIBUTION OF HNWIs AND THE VALUE OF PRIVATE WEALTH, 2000-2012

	HNWIs (million)			Value of private wealth (US$ trillion)		
	2000	2012	% growth	2000	2012	% growth
North America	2.2	3.7	+68	7.5	12.7	+69
Asia–Pacific	1.6	3.7	+131	4.8	12.0	+150
Europe	2.5	3.4	+36	8.4	10.9	+30
Latin America	0.3	0.5	+67	3.2	7.5	+134
Middle East	0.3	0.5	+67	1.0	1.8	+80
Africa	0.1	0.1	–	0.6	1.3	+117
Total	6.9	12.0	+74	25.5	46.2	+81

Source: Beaverstock and Wainwright (2013b). Reprinted with permission.

(CMLGWM, 2009). However, by 2009 the Asia–Pacific region, including Japan, became more important than Europe in terms of both the number of HNWIs and the amount of private wealth (see Table 5.2).

As a result, given the home bias of investors such that they typically prefer to locate in local markets, financial centres in Asia have rapidly been developing their private wealth management activities (Atkinson and Piketty, 2010; Piketty and Saez, 2014). Singapore and Hong Kong stand out in this respect. Both of these centres have sought to attract private wealth management investment by building on their established histories as leading IFCs and combining this with attractive regulatory and secrecy laws in order to attract the investment of private wealth.

THE CASE OF SINGAPORE AND HONG KONG AS MIDSHORE FINANCIAL CENTRES

In some ways it may seem surprising to focus on Singapore and Hong Kong as forms of offshore or midshore financial centres, since they are both well known as leading IFCs, and both consistently ranked as the third and fourth most significant such centres (see Table 2.1). This is built on their wider histories as commercial centres. In the case of Singapore this is based on its role as a trading centre within the British Empire, developed during the nineteenth century (Huat, 1987). This international focus was extended to include an increasingly vibrant domestic banking sector from the early 1900s, although its development as an IFC really took off following independence in 1965 as the government undertook deregulatory changes in order to attract international and commercial banks to the city state. Indeed, most of the major European, American and Japanese multinational banks opened offices in Singapore in the 1990s (Beaverstock and Doel, 2001).

Hong Kong initially shared a similar developmental trajectory because it was a major trading centre for the British Empire. However, the development of its international banking functions has included not only European and US banks, but also Chinese firms (see Meyer, 2000). As Hong Kong developed its manufacturing export-based industry from the 1950s, its banking and financial services sector developed to facilitate this industry, echoing the earlier development of other financial centres such as London in which financial services were based on an earlier export industry. Hong Kong matured into an IFC from the 1970s as an increasing number of multinational European, North American and Asian banks opened offices there. However, more recently, the development of Hong Kong has differed from that of Singapore. This difference can be largely accounted for through it becoming a Special Administrative Region within greater China. In this respect, while Hong Kong has maintained its reputation for being an outward-looking IFC, this is increasingly combined with its acting as an important site of policy experimentation as part of the wider internationalisation of the Chinese mainland economy.

However, in both cases, the private wealth management has played an important role in their continued development as financial centres. Because of the ways in which this industry relies upon privacy and certain forms of tax evasion (usually associated with offshore financial centres), coupled with dense and deep networks of financial services firms and legal services (more typically associated with IFCs), focusing on private wealth is helpful in terms of understanding how these centres can be considered as midshore financial centres. Indeed, figures show a considerable increase in the amount of private wealth being managed in each of the centres as they increasingly compete with more established European wealth and private banking sectors, notably Switzerland (Beaverstock et al., 2013a; 2013b; Long and Tan, 2010). For example, the growth rate of assets under management within private

TABLE 5.3 THE GROWTH OF TOTAL ASSETS UNDER MANAGEMENT (AuM) IN SINGAPORE, 2000-2012

Year	AuM (US$ bn)	Growth rate (US$ bn)	Percentage change
2000	276.2	+125.6	+46
2005	720.4	+444.2	+161
2006	891	+170.6	+24
2007	1,173	+452.6	+63
2008	864	−309	−26
2009	1,208	+344	+40
2010	1,354	+146	+13
2011	1,338	−16	−1
2012	1,626	+288	+22

Source: Beaverstock and Hall (2016)

wealth management between 1998 and 2012 in Singapore was 296 per cent (see Table 5.3). Approximately three-quarters of this private wealth under management comes from beyond Singapore, reflecting its role as an international private wealth management centre, with a particular reliance on wealth coming from the Asia–Pacific region (Beaverstock and Hall, 2016). This follows marked declines in assets under management coming from Europe and North America immediately after the 2007–2008 financial crisis. This reflects a concerted effort by the Singaporean monetary authorities to use regulation as a way of attracting the asset and fund management industry to Singapore, particularly that associated with private wealth management, in an effort to continue the development of the city as an IFC (Long and Tan, 2010).

A similar trend can be picked up in the figures for Hong Kong, although the way in which the Hong Kong monetary authorities collect their figures is different to Singapore's. The value of private banking assets under management in Hong Kong increased from 118 US$ bn in 2005 to 346 billion in 2012 (HKMA, 2013) with over half of these assets coming from Hong Kong itself and mainland China.

At one level the development of Singapore and Hong Kong, building on their previous role as commercial centres and their private wealth management industry based on attracting international clients, is important because of the ways in which it signals a change in the source of private wealth globally, moving away from established forms of inherited and dynastic wealth (Maude and Molyneux, 1996; Short, 2013) to new sources of wealth within Asia. It is also significant for the purposes of the arguments in this chapter that centre on understanding these locations as midshore financial centres. In this sense, the development of the private wealth management sector in both Singapore and Hong Kong needs to be understood by attending to their role as leading onshore IFCs as well the use of regulatory regimes and associated privacy laws that are more typical of OFCs (Beaverstock and Hall, 2016).

Taking the case of Singapore first, its development as a midshore financial centre, in which private wealth management plays an important role, relies on state support, particularly in terms of its taxation and regulatory policies, the broader attributes of Singapore as a leading IFC, and global supply and demand factors in terms of the sources of private wealth (Beaverstock and Hall, 2016). As for being an IFC, this means that the city has an established banking, financial and supporting professional services architecture that can service the private wealth management industry. This is coupled with characteristics that more closely resemble OFCs, particularly in terms of maintaining secrecy and the confidentiality of clients (Long and Tan, 2010). In addition, as regulation tightened up in Europe and North America in terms of privacy laws and regulations associated with private finance following the financial crisis, a number of private banks from Europe opened branches in Singapore. In addition, the financial services labour market in Singapore was well placed to support the development of its private banking sector, building on the highly skilled labour markets it uses as an IFC (Beaverstock, 2011).

As well as these infrastructure requirements to support the development of Singapore as a midshore financial centre, the city has also been able to capitalise on the increased demand for private banking services in Asia, associated with the growth of private wealth in Singapore itself in particular (Beaverstock and Hall, 2016). In this respect, in building on the growing dominance of the Asia–Pacific region as a source of private wealth, as discussed above, Singapore has been able to take advantage of home bias effects such that investors prefer to invest in geographically proximate markets in order to win, in effect, private sector banking business from other private banking centres in Europe and North America.

Again, the story is similar but with some nuances for the specifics of Hong Kong. Its development as a private banking sector rests partly on its role as an IFC, particularly in terms of its ability to attract highly skilled overseas finance professionals, and its favourable regulatory environment coupled with its unique position in relation to the Chinese economy. Indeed, the strength of Hong Kong as a genuinely 'international' IFC has been identified as one of the key factors in its development within private wealth management, which is argued to be more market driven rather than shaped considerably by deliberate state policy as in the case of Singapore (Long and Tan, 2010). This work identifies five important reasons for the development of Hong Kong as a private wealth management centre:

1   Its established position as a leading IFC with the associated supporting services such as international law firms as well as a significant cluster of leading international private banks like Coutts (from the UK), ABN AMRO (from the Netherlands), UBS (from Switzerland) and Deutsche Bank (from Germany). These twin strengths are attractive for private wealth customers because they allow individuals to choose from a range of products and there is an associated labour market in Hong Kong capable of successfully delivering such services.

2   Hong Kong has a strong legal and regulatory history as an IFC which helps foster trust-based relationships between both the providers and clients of the private wealth management industry. In particular, the Hong Kong legal system is underpinned by English Common Law, with some local adaptations, and this has been central in attracting overseas financial institutions to operate in the city.

3   While the above two factors draw on Hong Kong's strengths as an IFC, it can be characterised as a midshore financial centre, certainly in terms of its private wealth management industry, because it combines these strengths with banking secrecy laws that are more typical of offshore financial space. These include issues of personal data privacy within the Code of Banking Practices overseen by the Hong Kong monetary authorities. Given the nature of private wealth, maintaining confidentiality is an important factor for HNWIs, particularly when they are actively choosing to participate in low- or zero-tax activities,

and hence this enhances Hong Kong's attractiveness as a private wealth management centre.

4   These privacy laws are supported by a favourable tax regime in which the personal rate of taxation is 15 per cent and there is no value-added tax or sales tax and also no inheritance or death tax.

5   An important factor in the ongoing development of Hong Kong as a midshore private wealth management centre is its unique position vis-à-vis the mainland Chinese economy and particularly its significant role within the internationalisation of the Chinese economy (see Chapter 2). This is likely to stimulate further demand for private wealth management services as highly skilled individuals working in well-remunerated jobs continue to be attracted to work in RMB internationalisation within Hong Kong, but it will also offer the opportunity for the provision of innovative RMB-denominated products within the private wealth management industry.

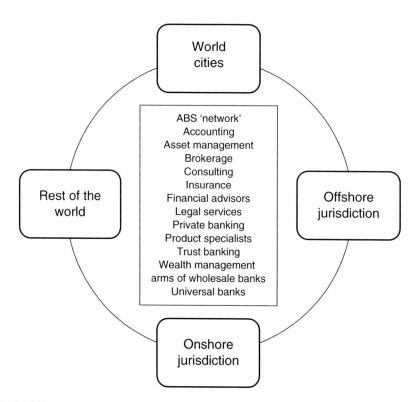

FIGURE 5.3   THE ABS OFFSHORE PRACTICE NETWORK AND NEXUS FOR PRIVATE WEALTH MANAGEMENT

Source: Beaverstock and Hall (2016). Reprinted with permission.

The cases of Singapore and Hong Kong therefore suggest that the offshore and onshore financial worlds need to be understood in relationship to each other as they are reproduced through a myriad of connections; these are shown, for the case of private wealth management, in Figure 5.3.

CONCLUSIONS

This chapter has focused upon the renewed interest in the offshore places and spaces within the international financial system in the wake of the 2007–2008 financial crisis. The study of offshore finance is by no means a new activity, although, despite a flurry of interest in the late 1990s and the early 2000s, relatively little attention was paid to offshore finance in the immediate run-up to the financial crisis beyond a small number of academics and non-governmental organisations concerned with promoting transparency in financial transactions (see for example Palan, 2006). For example, as discussed in Chapter 1, cultural economy approaches to money and finance were largely developed in the heartlands of global finance in the forms of IFCs in North America and Western Europe, rather than examining OFCs in detail. However, following the financial crisis, there has been a renewed interest in offshore finance within a range of social science disciplines, including economic geography, management studies, sociology and international relations.

This literature is important because it has significantly developed the theoretical and empirical scope and scale of research into offshore finance. Empirically, the research has documented a wider range of places within the global economy that are offering what would usually be seen as offshore financial services beyond the focus on small island economies and tax havens that characterised earlier work on OFCs. In particular, while studies of European and American OFCs have a longer history, it is now apparent that rapidly growing economies such as China are increasingly making use of offshore financial space through places such as the BVI (Haberly and Wójcik, 2015). This newer research has also drawn attention to the role of private wealth within the constitution of the offshore financial world, in addition to corporate wealth. Meanwhile, theoretically, by diversifying the range of studies of financial services and places within offshore finance, this research has increasingly sought to develop earlier relational approaches to the intersection between on- and offshore financial spaces by drawing attention to the rise of midshore financial centres that combine elements typically associated with both on- and offshore financial centres. In so doing, this research has also revealed the existence of offshore financial services activity within leading onshore financial centres such as London (Wainwright, 2011).

KEY FURTHER READINGS

Haberly, D. and Wójcik, D. (2015) Regional blocks and imperial legacies: mapping the global offshore FDI network. *Economic Geography*, 91(3): 251-280.

This paper provides a comprehensive overview of the changing geographies of offshore finance.

Roberts, S.M. (1995) Small place, big money: the Cayman Islands and the international financial system. *Economic Geography*, 71: 237–256.
This paper provides a detailed account of the nature of offshore island economies.

SECTION III

GLOBAL FINANCE AND FINANCIAL SUBJECTS

6

ELITES, FINANCIAL SUBJECTIVITIES AND THE (RE)PRODUCTION OF GLOBAL FINANCE

Chapter summary

- Rethinking financial elites
- Understanding elite financial subjects
  - *Understanding financial elites*
- The changing nature of elites in London's financial district
  - *Postgraduate education and investment-banking working cultures in London*
  - *(Re)producing quantitative finance through business education*
- Gendering financial elites
  - *Understanding the crisis in financial masculinity within London after the financial crisis*
- Conclusions

RETHINKING FINANCIAL ELITES

The popular imaginations that surrounded financiers prior to the financial crisis of 2007–2008 were dominated by images of young men aggressively pursuing their own personal financial ambitions in financial services. This group were frequently labelled in the media as 'masters of the universe', reflecting their perceived power within the global economy. However, this popular view was challenged during the financial crisis when these seemingly powerful individuals were pictured carrying out the much more mundane task of removing their personal effects from the high-rise investment bank offices in Canary Wharf in London and on Wall Street.

These images reflect the marked changes in investment banking business models following the crisis in which their approach to risk management and the circulation of debt through securitised finance from the USA to Western Europe was heavily criticised (Crotty, 2008). These developments came to a head when the previously leading US investment bank, Lehman Brothers, filed for bankruptcy in September 2008.

In the immediate aftermath of the crisis, in Western Europe and the USA, commercial banks, and bankers in particular, found themselves in the regulatory, political and media spotlight. This followed concern surrounding the extent to which governments had facilitated the continuation of investment banking by taking stakes in their balance sheets. One particular area of interest was bankers' pay and remuneration, with several jurisdictions bringing in legislation in an effort to limit this pay. For example, in January 2014 a 'bankers' bonus cap' was introduced within the EU which limited bankers' bonuses at 100 per cent of salary for the majority of bankers. Meanwhile, in the UK, there was a growing interest in separating what were seen as the risk-taking, 'casino'-type activities of investment banks from the utility functions of retail banking (The Vickers Report, 2013; for a fuller discussion of 'casino capitalism' see Strange, 1986, 1998).

However, despite this critical interest in investment banking business models and investment bankers themselves in the years immediately following the crisis, the financial services sector in IFCs such as London and New York has shown considerable regenerative capacity (Hall, 2009). For example, a range of new financial actors have emerged as becoming increasingly powerful in the face of the relative decline in the power of established investment banks, including private equity funds, hedge funds and sovereign wealth funds (Clark et al., 2013; Folkman et al., 2007). Indeed, these institutions have also lobbied for a more favourable regulatory environment for their activities, often threatening to relocate away from IFCs to offshore financial centres such as Switzerland in the case of Europe, although such claims have been higher on rhetoric than action. Meanwhile, some banks have increasingly threatened to use the increased banking regulation in Europe as a key factor in the possible relocation of their headquarters from London to Asia as in the case of HSBC and Standard Chartered Bank, both of which have considerable business interests in the Asia–Pacific region.

This chapter uses a focus on the changing nature of financial elites and investment bankers in particular, in the run-up to and fallout from the financial crisis, as a lens through which to view the changing nature of financial services practice within IFCs over the same time frame. This is achieved through a focus on the changing working practices, identities and subjectivities of investment bankers in London's financial district. The first section of the chapter begins by charting the growing interest in financial elites within the social sciences, particularly the contribution it can make to cultural economy approaches to finance. The second section of the chapter moves on to the case of London and examines the development of financial elite identities in London in the finance-led boom of the 2000s. This was a period that many academics and commentators argued had seen the rise of more meritocratic financial labour markets in which social and educational background became less important for financiers because individuals could potentially strategise about their educational and work experience decision making in order to secure entry into these labour markets (see for example Augar, 2009). However, in the second half of the chapter, the analysis reveals how financial elites working in London continue to embody particular gendered and classed subject positions, often derived from shared educational background at a limited number of universities. Indeed, the continued lack of access to such markets for individuals who have not been educated at a small number of leading universities has been the source of growing political interest in terms of wider agendas of equal opportunities and greater diversity within the professions (see for example The Cabinet Office, 2012). The concluding part of the chapter reflects on how focusing on individual bankers can advance cultural economy approaches to money and finance by revealing how individuals are inculcated into particular working practices that were central to both the causes and consequences of the financial crisis as well as the ongoing operation of the international financial system.

UNDERSTANDING ELITE FINANCIAL SUBJECTS

Elites have been widely identified as being central to the reproduction of the global economy and the international financial system in particular. For example, elites have been described as the choreographers of the corporate economies (Savage and Williams, 2008). Other phrases, including the transnational capitalist class, dominant managerial elites and new international professionals, have also been used to iden-tify the power held by elites in shaping the global economy (see, respectively, Sklair, 2001; Castells, 1996; Sassen, 2001 [1991]). However, these phrases point to the power of elites but leave a number of important questions unanswered. For example: What sort of work and activities do financial elites perform and how does this give them structural power? How do individuals assume the position of elites? Are elites as homogeneous and globally influential as these labels suggest?

Moreover, these questions have remained comparatively neglected within the social science literature because the study of elites has not been widely undertaken. In part this reflects a reticence among critical social scientists to study elites for fear of becoming complicit in their power or enhancing their agency within the global economy (Savage and Williams, 2008). Indeed, the cultural economy literature rec-ognises that it is the combination of human and non-human actors that needs to be understood in order to examine the making of financial markets. However, while this literature examines how non-human actors, particularly financial theories, are assembled and used in financial markets, comparatively little attention has been paid to how human actors are assembled and positioned as important actors in shaping financial markets (Hall, 2012; for a notable exception on financial subjectivities on Wall Street, see Ho, 2009). This neglect is in contrast to recent research in retail finance that has begun to consider how the *consumers* of financial products are (re)produced through a variety of educational and learning experiences (see for example Leyshon et al., 1998). This work is instructive since it responds to calls for greater attention to political questions within cultural economy (see Pryke and Du Gay, 2007) by interrogating the *types* of financial subjectivities being reproduced, a point we return to in our conclusions.

Indeed, in many ways the neglect of understanding the nature of financial elites is surprising, given the ways in which having a ready supply of highly skilled individuals has been seen as central to the successful reproduction of IFCs. For example, a ready supply of such individuals is used by the consultancy firm Z/Yen as a key metric within its annual rankings of IFCs (see for example Z/Yen, 2015). Meanwhile, policy makers with responsibility for supporting and promoting particular IFCs are also well aware of the need for a ready supply of these people. For example, the then Lord Mayor of the City of London, John Stuttard, stated in 2006 that:

> The success of any financial market depends on its people and their skill base. London is the prime international financial and business services centre in the world because of the size and competence of its skilled workforce. … During my mayoralty I will be using my programme of overseas visits to promote these services. … In this way we will be able to achieve an even greater profile around the world for the City of London as the City of Learning.

However, following interventions that emphasise the need for social scientists to demonstrate 'a reengagement with fundamental questions about elites and the organizational infrastructures they operate in' (Zald and Lounsbury, 2010: 964; see also Engelen et al., 2012), scholars have more recently positioned elites more centrally within work on financial services (Savage and Williams, 2008).

UNDERSTANDING FINANCIAL ELITES

Financial elites have been widely identified as an important component in shaping the variegated nature of the international financial system and the geographically distinctive ways in which financial services markets are made in different IFCs (see Clark and Wójcik, 2007; Dixon, 2011; Engelen et al., 2010; Faulconbridge and Muzio, 2009). This approach has received particular attention following the financial crisis as the institutional landscape of London's financial district has been closely examined because of the role it may have played in legitimating the production and use of certain financial products that have subsequently been identified as being central to causing the financial crisis (Tett, 2009). The approach emphasises the ways in which an individual's expertise and working practices are shaped, at least in part through the embedded economies in which they work. For example, these place-specific qualities play an important role in shaping what counts as acceptable, desirable work behaviours, dress codes and the like so that other forms of action are prevented from taking place (Zald and Lounsbury, 2010: 972). This approach acknowledges that different financial centres will have different cultures; however, it has much less to say on how these different cultures emerge, how they are reproduced and how they change over time (Faulconbridge and Hall, 2014). A focus on how individuals are inculcated into working as financial elites within different financial services provides one way of addressing this oversight.

In this respect a focus on how education and training are used to produce in effect individuals who embody certain working practices has been used to try to address this oversight. There has been a growing interest in the use of education to produce certain kinds of elites, building on the identification of a 'cultural circuit of capital' (Thrift, 2005) that produces the knowledge and resources deployed by managers and other highly skilled workers in addition to educating individuals about the value of this knowledge. This circuit is made up of business schools (particularly their MBA programmes), management consultants and business gurus, and it emerged in response to the increasingly uncertain global space economy from the 1960s onwards. It has been central in circulating and legitimating a new managerial discourse that emphasises the need for greater flexibility, adaptability and reflexivity from both organisations and individuals. Of particular importance for the arguments in this chapter are the ways in which business education not only circulates particular types of technical know-how and competencies, but also engineers and assembles 'new, more appropriate kinds of *subjects*, what we might call "souls" that fit contemporary and especially future systems of accumulation' (Thrift and Olds, 2004: 274, italics in original). The range of educational activities involved in facilitating entry into and upward mobility within elite financial labour markets is summarised in Table 6.1.

TABLE 6.1 LONDON'S FINANCIAL BUSINESS EDUCATION LANDSCAPE

Financial expertise	Type of education/ training	Dominant financial education	Indicative education providers
'Calculatives devices' (Callon, 1998)	Non-regulatory training	PhD Msc in Finance Joint intiatives between universities and financial institutes Specialist for-profit education boutiques	University MScs Oxford-Man Institute of Quantitative Finance 7city
'knowledge … concerned with subjectification' (Olds and Thrift, 2005)	Management development, interpersonal skills/team working, communication, sales/customer service	For-profit education companies and consultancies MBA programmes Sole-operated coaching and mentoring	JMW Consultants Lane4
Regulatory clearance	Regulatory and compliance	Accredited for-profit education companies	BPP Professional Education Kaplan Financial

Source: Hall and Appleyard (2009) Reprinted with permission from Oxford University Press. Permission conveyed through Copyright Clearance Centre, Inc.

In terms of understanding how this circuit inculcates financiers into particular ways of being and working, the work of the sociologist Pierre Bourdieu on elite formation beyond the case of finance is instructive. Bourdieu (1990; 1996) understands action, in this case the operation of financial services in particular IFCs, as being located in fields, each of which has assumptions as to what would count as appropriate thoughts and actions within that field (Faulconbridge and Muzio, 2009; Sassen, 2012). These socio-cultural dimensions to IFCs shape and help produce the distinctive working cultures which are associated with different financial centres (Amin and Thrift, 1992; Augar, 2001; Cook et al., 2012; Hanlon, 2004). In order to understand how these fields are reproduced through the action of individuals, a focus on education and training is useful because it draws attention to the types of practices that become legitimated in particular financial centres. In this respect, Bourdieu's work can be expanded by drawing on the growing interest in the nature of social and economic practice within the social sciences (see Gherardi, 2009; Jones and Murphy, 2011; Reckwitz, 2002; Røpke, 2009; Shove, 2003; Wenger 1998; Wilk, 2002).

Three components of social practice have been identified (Shove et al., 2012). First, and following the broader work on cultural economy approaches to financial markets, practices involve humans interacting with a range of non-human or technological actors. Second, the use of these technologies is partly shaped by the cultural aspects of individual actors so that they are motivated to use certain technologies, such as a particular approach to valuing a company, above others, because of the personal benefits and increase in personal status that may accrue from this usage (on the rise of quantitative valuation cultures within investment banks, see Hall, 2006). Third, in order to be able to deploy technologies to such ends, however, an individual needs to demonstrate particular competencies which combine the technical know-how associated with a particular technology, as well as the acknowledgement and more subtle understanding, about when using a technology or valuation technique would be particularly valuable and when and where it may not be deemed legitimate (see Table 6.2). Research on financial elites has begun to use these insights to understand the role of education and training in shaping both the technical know-how and more experiential knowledge required to act and work in certain ways in different financial centres. It is in this way that education and training can begin to be seen as an important set of activities in (re)producing the different working cultures associated with different financial centres as well as facilitating the flow of knowledge and information between them (Faulconbridge and Hall, 2014; Hall and Appleyard, 2009; 2011).

The rest of this chapter uses these theoretical approaches to chart the ways in which postgraduate education can be used as a lens to examine the changing nature of what counts as a legitimate financial elite within London in the run-up to and following the financial crisis. In so doing, the analysis demonstrates how focusing on financial elites provides a valuable way of developing understandings of the specific working cultures that emerge in particular financial centres and the implications of these for variegation between IFCs and the international financial system more generally.

TABLE 6.2 FORMS OF KNOWLEDGE AND PRACTICES OF KNOWING INVOLVED IN USING THE DISCOUNTED CASH FLOW MODEL WITHIN CORPORATE FINANCE

Type of knowledge/ practices of knowing	Indicative example quote from research interviews	Potential mobility between MBA classrooms and corporate finance practice
'Functional Knowledge' (Thrift and Olds, 2004)	'The theory is a scientific fact and that travels relatively easily' (Associate Professor, Chicago GSB, March 2006)	High
Geographically contingent knowledges	'There are norms about how you would apply the DCF, say if you were looking at an M&A in China, compared to a mature market like, say France' (Assistant Professor, Cass Business School, March 2007)	Moderately high
Firm 'best practice' (Gertler, 2001)	'There are bank norms as to what discount rate they apply so trying to tell someone from Goldmans [Goldman Sachs] that that is just a corporate policy and that there are other options is a real challenge' (Professor, London Business School, December 2006)	Low
Embodied expertise	'When I'm looking at a bid, yes there is the mechanics from business school but sometimes you just have a look at something, and you have a feeling, an approach just feels right ... I don't know how you would teach that in the classroom' (Harvard MBA, 2004) investment bank vice-president, London, March 2007	Low

Source: Hall (2008)

THE CHANGING NATURE OF ELITES IN LONDON'S FINANCIAL DISTRICT

Although a focus on financial elites has not been central to understanding the development of financial centres within a cultural economy perspective, two strands of work on IFCs can be identified that do signal the importance of attending to elites (see also Chapter 2). First, attention has been paid to understanding how developing interpersonal relations among financiers within and between IFCs is vital to the production and circulation of technical know-how which is central to the creation of financial products and the ability to tailor these to the demands of corporate clients (Clark and O'Connor, 1997). Indeed, the importance of such relations has led to a whole set of mobility practices within investment banking labour markets, including short but frequent forms of business travel between financial centres as well as expatriation and longer forms of migration. Second, this research emphasises that technical know-how is not the only form of knowledge that is important within financial services work. Rather, this is accompanied by forms of know-how that are typically more embodied in nature and give rise to the importance of particular bodily performances among financiers in London (Hall and Appleyard, 2009; Thrift, 1994).

In order to develop these insights through the case of London, this chapter works with an understanding of working cultures. These working cultures comprise the taken-for-granted assumptions shaped by both firms and financial centres that define what legitimate forms of working activities, knowledge practices and interpersonal relations are in any given working context. From the mid-twentieth century, the working culture in London is typically captured through the term 'gentlemanly capitalism' (Augar, 2001). This term reflected the ways in which merchant banking, which was the dominant banking business model at the time, comprised labour markets that were highly gendered numerically both in terms of the under-repre-sentation of women and in terms of how certain performances of masculinity were privileged. Moreover, recruitment and education were also an important component of these working cultures as individuals were typically recruited through shared social and educational backgrounds at a small number of elite public (fee-paying) schools and the Universities of Oxford and Cambridge. The resulting 'old boys' networks' (Cain and Hopkins, 1987; Michie, 1992) were used not only for recruitment pur-poses, but also as a way of developing the trust-based relations that were central to the merchant banking business model in which clients typically developed long-standing relationships and loyalty with one bank, and used this bank for all their banking requirements rather than engaging a range of banks as is more typical in the investment banking business model. As Thrift (1994: 342) notes, this 'narrative of the gentleman' was 'based on values of honour, integrity, courtesy and so on, and manifested in ideas of how to act, ways to talk [and] suitable clothing' (see also Tickell, 1996). Research has demonstrated how multiple masculinities existed in the City in the 1990s as the 'gentlemen' of merchant banks were accompanied by an increasingly aggressive macho masculinity associated with traders (McDowell, 1997). Nevertheless, it remains the case that the narrative of the gentleman was particularly important. Indeed, it has been argued that 'gentlemanly capitalism' underpinned London's historically light-touch approach to regulation in which the Bank of England was located within close proximity to the banks it was regulating such that the Bank could use this to fulfil its regulatory requirements based on a shared understanding between financiers and the Bank that a 'gentleman's word was his bond' (see Pryke, 1991).

Initially, the internationalisation of financial institutions in London from the 1990s onwards had relatively little effect on the working practices of wholesale bankers, and work tended to focus on established (US) investment banking activities including corporate finance activities, particularly offering advice to corporations on M&As. However, as described in more detail in Chapter 2, during the late 1990s and 2000s the profitability of this business model was challenged, leading to the develop-ment of alternative investment banking business models. Folkman et al. (2007) go on to argue that, as a result, investment bankers are one component group of 'new capitalized markets' or what are termed elsewhere 'financialised elites', 'who play a significant role in shaping processes of financialisation by not simply servicing the financial and banking requirements of large corporations but also increasingly by operating in financial markets in their own right' (Hall, 2009: 179).

This shift has led to a marked change in the working practices of London's financial district banking community. Previously, investment banking was a relationship-based business as banks worked to develop long-term relationships with commercial clients. However, during the late 1990s, the nature of investment banking itself changed as, for example, undertaking an M&A transaction increasingly involved not a bilateral relationship between a bank and a corporate client, but centred on managing the relationships between a number of financial institutions, including corporate finance boutiques, hedge funds and corporate law firms, all of which have become increasingly important in delivering the increasingly bespoke financial advice demanded by corporate clients (Folkman et al., 2007; Hall, 2007). These working practices within investment banks changed even more markedly with the rise of structured finance, particularly securitisation during the 2000s. This form of financial services work led to growing demand for individuals who were highly numerate, often holding postgraduate degrees in subjects such as maths, physics and computer science, such that these individuals could perform 'socio-financial engineering' (Pryke and Allen, 2000) in which complex structured finance products were developed that offered 'the allure of high potential margins at a corporate level and personal remuneration through bonuses at the individual level' (Hall, 2009: 184).

This changed working culture, which is typified by a greater emphasis on technical and quantitative know-how rather than relation-based services, has been widely identified and debated, not least in terms of how it in part caused the international financial crisis (Tett, 2009). However, comparatively less attention has been paid to how this working culture was produced and sustained in London. In this respect, a number of factors are important, including the changing make-up of London's financial district in terms of the types of firms operating there and the regulatory environment that favoured and permitted certain forms of financial services activity. However, in what follows, we return to the long-standing relationship between education and London's working culture, to suggest that this represents an important but comparatively neglected set of activities and practices that shape the working cultures of the City.

POSTGRADUATE EDUCATION AND INVESTMENT-BANKING WORKING CULTURES IN LONDON

The rise in quantitative finance associated with the changing investment banking business models and the growth of securitisation in the 2000s has been accompanied by some marked changes in the relationship between educational background and investment banking labour markets. While education at a limited number of elite universities remains an important factor in securing entry into these labour markets, it has been accompanied by a proliferation of postgraduate education and early-career training which is increasingly seen as necessary in order to position oneself successfully to secure employment in the City (Hall and Appleyard, 2009; see also Table 6.3). For example, recruits increasingly hold master's degrees, often in quantitative skills, or obtain an MBA later on in their career in order to maximise their positional advantage relative to other employees. This generic education is typically

TABLE 6.3   PERCENTAGE OF BANKERS ENGAGED IN TRAINING AND EDUCATION DIVIDED BY CAREER LEVEL, 2007

Type of training/education	Managerial and senior managerial banking staff (%)	Professional and technical banking staff (%)
Regulatory and compliance	71	49
Non-regulatory training	27	76
Management development	90	36
Interpersonal skills/team working	60	58
Communication	88	67
Sales/customer service	35	58

Source: Hall and Appleyard (2009) Reprinted with permission from Oxford University Press. Permission conveyed through Copyright Clearance Centre, Inc.

accompanied by firm-specific training, including graduate training schemes in which individuals work for a small period of time across a number of banking functions. Recent work in economic geography has begun to explore the importance of these educational activities not only in facilitating entry into elite labour markets, but also in (re)producing the distinctive working cultures of particular IFCs (Faulconbridge and Hall, 2014). This approach draws on theories of practice to explore how economic practices are situated and normalised in particular geographical and institutional settings (see Gherardi, 2009; Shove, 2003). In particular, through a focus on London's early-career financial and legal elite Faulconbridge and Hall examine 'how post-first-degree education represents an important means by which early-career elites are inculcated into the place-specific and organizationally specific meanings, competencies and technologies associated with financial business practices' (2014: 1683).

The internationalisation of the City from the 1990s onwards, associated with the rise of new financial products, notably structured finance, meant that historic ways of recruiting bankers through 'old boys' networks' associated with a small number of schools could no longer meet the demands of the City's labour markets (Leyshon and Thrift, 1997). This led to a widening of the educational backgrounds of those recruited into the City, albeit in only a limited way as recruitment became increasingly focused on the UK's elite Russell Group of universities (Jones, 1998). However, as the number of graduates seeking entry into these labour markets also grew, recruitment into financial services in the City became increasingly typified by positional competitions as individuals sought to obtain higher degrees and additional credentials in order to secure access, as well as undertaking internships (Hall and Appleyard, 2009). Indeed, in many ways the growing importance of an internship in securing employment in a leading investment bank is evidence of the ways in which vestiges of 'gentlemanly capitalism' remain, since these openings are sometimes not widely advertised and are arranged by the personal and familial contacts of students wanting to undertake one. Moreover, they are often not paid or, if they are, only nominally, and as such, undertaking an internship is limited to those with enough financial support to live in London.

This has given rise to a variegated financial business education landscape in the City in which three main types of providers exist (Hall and Appleyard, 2009). First, despite concerns surrounding MBA degrees, universities remain important in offering education to financiers working in the City, increasingly expanding their range of business education courses beyond MBA degrees to include more specialist master's degrees, particularly those in quantitative finance. Second, for-profit specialist business education firms have become increasingly significant actors. This part of the educational landscape is dominated by large multinational education and training companies. These multinationals are increasingly accompanied by small, specialist, educational boutiques that deal in a particular type of financial services education, for example quantitative finance. Third and finally, for graduates beginning work in investment banks, these multinationals also offer graduate training schemes for junior staff and more bespoke ongoing educational opportunities for more senior staff.

On the face of it, these developments might suggest that London's financial district had become more meritocratic, with an individual's educational background at a small number of elite schools and universities becoming less important because the individual could secure entry into and upward mobility within financial labour markets through the appropriate investment in ongoing education. However, research has shown that while not necessarily reproducing the established forms of gentlemanly capitalism that have characterised London's financial labour markets in the past, these ongoing forms of business education play an important part in legitimating particular forms of action and behaviour that shape London's financial labour markets in particular ways (Hall, 2013). One of these is considered in more detail below: the ways in which business education is used to reproduce quantitatively literate financiers capable of designing, reproducing, circulating and selling the financial products that were at the heart of the financial crisis.

(RE)PRODUCING QUANTITATIVE FINANCE THROUGH BUSINESS EDUCATION

The ability to act as a technically skilled financier is not a new requirement within financial labour markets in the City. Discourses of order and control that surround technical know-how echo elements of the idealised 'gentlemanly capitalist', particularly the 'corporate finance patriarch' who was 'sober, rational and powerful' (McDowell, 1997: 182). However, a key difference between these earlier discourses of rationality and control associated with technical competency and the quantitative investment banker in the 2000s lies in the dense web of relations between education providers and investment banks used to produce, legitimate and circulate a discourse of 'smartness' (Ho, 2009).

Research has shown how education plays an important role in the reproduction of this 'culture of smartness' on Wall Street through close relationships between investment banks and a limited number of Ivy League universities in the USA (Ho, 2009). Following the findings of this research, discourses of 'smartness' and 'talent' are central to the self-identification of investment bankers in the City. For example, the 2011 graduate recruitment campaign run by the investment banking arm of the UK bank Barclays, Barclays Capital, was based around the slogan 'See yourself working alongside the best in the business' (Barclays Capital, 2012).

However, while educational background serves as a marker of entry into this self-defined 'globally talented' labour market, ongoing education is also central to the reproduction of discourses about the intellectual ability of bankers in London. In particular, these discourses emphasise the need for investment bankers to act in rational and calculative ways so that they could convert their technical know-how into income streams, both for themselves in terms of their own remuneration packages and for their employing investment banks (O'Neill, 2009).

In some ways, this focus on the development of quantitative financial skills might be seen as the start of more progressive financial labour markets in which educational background becomes less important and individuals are able to secure entry to and upward mobility within these labour markets by acquiring the desirable skills that are rewarded within a more quantitative-finance-dominated investment banking business model. However, as Thrift reminds us:

> For all the commitment to an open-ended view of subjecthood, in practice, the conception of the person (and the model of action) that is presumed is, more often than not, a narrow one. (2005: 47)

Indeed, reports continue to document the importance of educational background in securing entry into professional labour markets in countries such as the UK, including financial services. In what follows, one such form of continuation between 'gentlemanly capitalism' and more recent working cultures in London's financial district is explored, focusing on the gendered nature of financial labour markets.

GENDERING FINANCIAL ELITES

The gendered nature of financial elite labour markets remains a key factor in understanding the (re)production of elite financial subjectivities. Indeed the persistent ways in which access to what are deemed to be legitimate subjectivities within highly skilled labour markets continues to be restricted to certain social and cultural groups (see for example McDowell, 2010). These debates have been developed most fully through work that identifies the *multiple* masculinities that are associated with discourses of 'gentlemanly capitalism' (McDowell, 1997). This work identifies two particularly significant masculinities that have dominated London's financial labour markets, historically at least: first, the financial patriarch embodying the qualities usually associated with 'gentlemanly capitalism', including rationality, order and control, in ways that echo the earlier discussion of quantitative financial skills; and, second, the exuberant trade embodying optimism, confidence and enthusiasm. The salience of this analysis is reflected in the ways in which these masculinities are also reflected in accounts of working in financial services from previous industry insiders.

For example, the first mortgage-backed securities transactions by Salomon Brothers in the mid-1980s were led by traders who were commonly known as 'big swinging dicks' – a highly gendered phrase used to describe the aggressive tactics of the most profitable traders (Lewis, 1989). Meanwhile, ethnographic work on Wall

Street has revealed the gendered nature of internal labour markets within banks, with senior positions in front office activities such as corporate finance, sales and trading and asset management being dominated by men, while women and people of colour dominate the far less lucrative back office support functions such as trade reconciliation and technical support (Ho, 2009).

These studies of the long-standing gendered nature of financial services work are instructive because they develop a further strand of cultural economy research that focuses more on the discursive constitution of financial markets and their activity associated with representations of finance in the popular consciousness, the media and organisational and city-specific working cultures (see De Goede, 2005; Langley, 2008). However, despite discourses being identified as an important way of legitimising certain (gendered) working practices while de-legitimising others, less attention has been paid to precisely how individuals are inculcated into these discourses. This oversight comes despite individuals who used to work in finance acknowledging the ways in which training courses within investment banks, for example, were important in their learning the gendered norms of their employing organisations during their careers (Lewis, 2010).

This oversight is particularly significant, given the ways in which gendered understandings of financial elites became central to understandings of financial labour markets in the immediate aftermath of the financial crisis in IFCs such as London.

UNDERSTANDING THE CRISIS IN FINANCIAL MASCULINITY WITHIN LONDON AFTER THE FINANCIAL CRISIS

Understanding the challenges posed to financial masculinity and the ways in which individuals were educated in particular subjectivities took on a renewed importance in London, given the persistent stream of discrimination cases brought by women against their financial services firms' employers as well as high-profile policy documents that seek to offer possible solutions for improving the career opportunities of women working in financial services (Treasury Committee, 2010). These concerns were given more publicity in the immediate aftermath of the financial crisis in London as politicians, policy makers and the general public sought explanations for why the crisis happened. Questions were asked as to whether hyper-masculine investment bankers who embodied the traits of 'masters of the universe' (Wolfe, 1987), and were prepared to take significant risks because of their faith in their analytical and quantitative financial skills as discussed above, were to blame. Consequently, this form of 'testosterone capitalism' (McDowell, 2010) found itself in the political and public spotlight, with a number of critics going so far as to suggest that, had a greater number of female financiers been employed, associated with what these popular accounts identified as essentialised feminine traits of long-term care and nurturing, then this would have prevented the crisis.

Moreover, while the quantitative financial education discussed above aimed to produce highly rational, decisive, masculine subjectivities, research has shown that our understandings of financial crises themselves are highly gendered because emotion can never be totally teased out of financial services labour markets (De Goede, 2005; Langley, 2008; McDowell, 1997). In particular, financial crises themselves have been understood in gendered ways historically as moments of irrationality, as opposed to the usually 'ordered' nature of finance:

> gendered representations of financial crises as instances of madness, delusion, hysteria and irrationality have had particular historical durability, which simultaneously constructs the sphere of financial normality or rationality. (De Goede, 2005: 39)

As such, the financial crisis was unusual in being framed, initially at least, as a crisis of financial masculinity, as evidenced by images of typically male financiers who had been seen as seemingly untouchable in terms of their economic power – 'masters of the universe' lining up at bank offices in Canary Wharf when redundancies were announced and subsequently seen carrying their personal effects out of these offices. At this point in the crisis, at least initially, these images contributed to framing the crisis as the inability of supposedly rational and calculative investment bankers to manage the more emotive aspects of financial services work as they became increasingly divorced from more common-sense understandings of economic practice and engaged in what were framed as excessive, rather than calculative, risk-taking activities. In other words, the crisis was being scripted, at least in part, as a crisis of the masculinity of the investment banker subject. This analysis went further, with commentators actively suggesting that the crisis could have potentially been avoided if more women had been employed, as the financial commentator Ros Altman claimed:

> Women have a caring mind-set, a nurturing mind-set, a mind-set that says let's worry about the future. What's happened at the top of institutions and in the economy as a whole has been very different from that. It has been very much instant gratification. I know you can't generalise, but there is a gender difference in outlook, whether it is because of the nurturing role mothers play. What has driven these men has been short-termism and irresponsibility. (2009: 25)

These arguments were echoed in policy reports on financial services by the Treasury Committee when investigating the under-representation of women in the City in the wake of the crisis:

> There is a consensus that an effective challenge function within a board is required in financial institutions, and that diversity on boards can promote such challenge. While it is impossible to know whether more female board members would have lessened the impact of the financial crisis, the arguments for fairness, improved corporate governance, a stronger challenge function and not wasting a large proportion of talent seem more than sufficient to conclude that increased gender diversity is desirable. (2010: 12)

At one level, this more high-profile debate about the continued gendered nature of financial services work and the under-representation of women within it can be welcomed as part of wider work addressing the lack of meritocracy within highly skilled financial labour markets. However, an important caveat needs to be made. In this respect, investment banks and the wholesale financial services sector in the UK have been remarkably successful in framing the crisis as an irrational aberration in ways that echo more long-standing debates about how crises are framed as a deviation from the norm. For financial institutions and banks, this is important because it has allowed them to position themselves as returning to 'business as usual' far more quickly than many commentators had expected (French and Leyshon, 2010). While this has made debates concerning meaningful reform to the international financial system significantly harder, it does demonstrate how (gendered) representations of finance and associated performances of financial knowledge are intricately entwined with questions of power (Langley, 2008), particularly given the ways in which UK governments continue to be wary of critiquing the City, and investment banks in particular, for fear that they will relocate outside the UK.

This analysis, focusing on the performance of gendered discourses of who a successful financier could or should be at different stages both during and after the crisis, offers one way of developing a more politically engaged cultural economy that seeks to understand how particular financial behaviours became normalised in the 2000s and, subsequently, how financiers have framed the crisis as a relatively discrete, abnormal event, turning the focus instead towards public-sector efficiencies, national deficits and the economics of austerity.

CONCLUSIONS

This chapter has focused on the making of elite financial subjects who are central to the (re)production of global finance. This topic is both empirically and theoretically significant. First, empirically, much has been made of the potential decline in the importance of educational and social background in terms of securing entry into and upward mobility within elite financial labour markets. In particular, the greater emphasis on education and training for individuals who are working in these labour markets potentially signals the development of a more meritocratic financial services labour market in London in which individuals can progress, based not on their gender or background, but on the strategic acquisition of particular skills, notably quantitative financial ones. However, the research reported in this chapter demonstrates how some of the exclusionary values associated with financial services work that lay at the heart of discourses of 'gentlemanly capitalism' still persist. The chapter has examined the continued gendered nature of these labour markets and the role of women in them. In this respect, while the 2007–2008 financial crisis initially proved a moment in which these gendered elements were clearly revealed, this period of critical reflection about the type of gendered work being conducted in financial services in London quickly shut down, with financial institutions themselves using this as a way of attempting to return to business as usual as quickly as possible after the crisis. As a result, debates continue surrounding the gendered nature of financial services work and the implications of this for the development of less heavily gendered financial labour markets, in common with similar debates that are taking place in policy-making circles about highly skilled graduate labour markets more generally.

Theoretically, the chapter expands the cultural economy research agenda pursued through the book in important ways. Most notably, the focus on multiple agents involved in market making that has dominated much of the cultural economy literature, and which has been the primary focus of the book so far, has had relatively little to say about how individuals are assembled within financial markets and the implications of this for both individuals and markets. In order to address this, the chapter turns to a different strand of cultural economy research that emphasises the discursive construction of financial markets (De Goede, 2005; Langley, 2010). This work is valuable because it examines how discourses legitimate particular forms of financial action. However, the chapter has argued that this work could be developed further by attending to the ways in which individuals become inculcated into such discourses, particularly through different forms of education. Moreover, this approach is useful in revealing the similarities as well as the differences between contemporary financial labour markets and previous generations working in financial centres such as London. This chapter has focused on the (re)production of gendered understandings of who counts as a successful financier and particularly the gendered forms of action that these individuals are encouraged to undertake. In so doing, this approach to cultural economy provides a valuable way of using the study of individuals working at the heart of the international financial system to reveal the important power relations that underpin global finance. This is an important contribution since the wider cultural economy literature has been criticised for its lack of focus on questions of politics and power.

KEY FURTHER READINGS

Folkman, P., Froud, J., Johal, S. and Williams, K. (2007) Working for themselves? Capital market intermediaries and present day capitalism. *Business History*, 49: 552–572.
This paper sets out the changing nature of financial elites in the wake of the 2007–2008 financial crisis.

Hall, S. and Appleyard, L. (2009) 'City of London, City of Learning'? Placing business education within the geographies of finance. *Journal of Economic Geography*, 9: 597–617.
This paper sets out the relationship between business education and financiers working in London's international financial district.

McDowell, L. (1997) *Capital Culture*. Oxford: Blackwell.
This book provides a pathbreaking analysis of the gendered nature of financial labour markets in London.

7

FINANCIAL EXCLUSION AND EVERYDAY FINANCIAL SUBJECTS

Chapter summary

- Everyday finance

- Understanding the intersection between individuals, households and the international financial system

- Variegated 'investor subjects' within the international financial system

  o Variegated pension planning in financial markets in the UK

  o Variegated life insurance in financial markets in the UK

- Financial exclusion and the everyday life of financialisation

  o The geographies of financial exclusion

  o Causes of financial exclusion

  o From financial exclusion to redlining and sub-prime finance

- Conclusions

EVERYDAY FINANCE

Although financialisation is often seen as a process being driven from leading financial centres, a key insight of research into financialisation is a recognition of the ways in which individuals, households and firms have become increasingly tied into the international financial system in the run-up to and fallout from the 2007–2008 financial crisis through a process termed 'the financialisation of everyday life' (Martin, 2002). For example, an individual's pension provision, and hence their livelihood in old age, is increasingly tied into the fortunes of financial markets, and stock markets in particular (see Clark, 2003). This follows the decline in defined benefit pensions, such as final salary pension schemes in which individuals and employers made regular payments into a pension scheme that would then guarantee a pension value, normally expressed as a percentage of the individual's salary on retirement. In its place, pensions schemes in many Western European and North American economies are more commonly defined contribution schemes in which individuals and employers contribute a designated amount which then is used to develop a pension fund. The value of this fund on retirement is determined by the fortunes of the stock market. Meanwhile, the ability of individuals to purchase homes is determined increasingly by their ability to secure mortgage finance. And yet, it was the rapid increase in rates and associated defaults associated with this in certain segments of the mortgage market that was central to initially causing the financial crisis, as discussed in Chapter 4.

Focusing on the experience of the international financial system by households and individuals is particularly important following the financial crisis because, while wholesale finance within IFCs has demonstrated remarkable regenerative capabilities such that global finance continues its centrality within the global economy, individuals and households have encountered the uneven financial and geographical outcomes of the crisis. For example, with respect to mortgage finance, while the wealthier sections of many advanced economies have enjoyed the benefits associated with an unprecedented period of prolonged low interest rates, reducing their mortgage repayments, those living in low-income and minority neighbourhoods have encountered an increase in mortgage default (foreclosure) rates and associated problems of financial exclusion in securing access to basic financial products and services (Aalbers, 2009a; 2009b).

Although cultural economy research that focuses on the making of wholesale financial markets as discussed in Chapters 2 and 6 has not been widely applied to understandings of individuals as financial consumers, a broader literature has developed that examines the implications of the deepening of financial relations between individuals and the international financial system (see for example Langley, 2008). This work emphasises how individuals are not only tied into the international financial system through a range of financial products, but also encouraged to act in particular ways in order to participate within this mode of economic governance. Particular attention has been focused on how individuals are increasingly positioned as 'investor subjects' who are encouraged to strategise about their own financial decision making in order to ensure their own financial security, in essence acting increasingly like professional financial advisors. In so doing, this work positions financialisation within the broader retreat of the welfare state in several advanced economies, particularly under the political conditions of austerity that have prevailed following the financial crisis. Under this austerity politics, several governments have sought to cut public services radically in an effort to reduce what is perceived to be inflated state spending that is contributing to significant public sector deficits (Langley, 2014).

This chapter begins by examining the different ways in which the relationship between individual households and the international financial system has been theorised. Particular attention is drawn to the ways in which the variegated nature of such relationships has been comparatively neglected (French and Kneale, 2009). In order to address this, the second and third sections of the chapter focus on addressing this lacuna by focusing particularly on financial products and the uneven nature of financial exclusion, respectively.

UNDERSTANDING THE INTERSECTION BETWEEN INDIVIDUALS, HOUSEHOLDS AND THE INTERNATIONAL FINANCIAL SYSTEM

The most important literature that has developed in order to understand how individuals have increasingly become tied into the international financial system, and the uneven outcomes of this for financial consumers, is by focusing on the ways in which particular financial subjects are created through and within the international financial system via a range of financial activities related to, for example, pension planning, mortgage finance and life insurance (Langley, 2007; 2008; see also Larner, 2007). This literature takes as its starting point Foucault's (1979) work on governmentality to examine how the international financial system calls forth particular forms of financial subjects such that individuals in many advanced capitalist economies have increasingly been positioned as being responsible for 'managing' their own financial practices in ways that conform to wider discourses of the importance of personal responsibility and risk management that are embedded within neoliberal financial markets and economic policies more generally (Langley, 2007; 2008).

In part, this use of neo-Foucauldian governmentality approaches reflects the ways in which such work has become increasingly significant within understandings of the global economy more generally and within critical social sciences beyond the specific case of money and finance (Dean, 1999). For example, valuable insights into the processes of globalisation have been developed by examining how the global is not a pre-existing state, disembedded from socio-economic practices, but is (re)produced through a range of political discourses and programmes that enrol both socio-technical calculative devices and individual actors (see Amin, 2002; Larner, 2007; Larner and Walters, 2005). In terms of work on finance in particular, this literature has been used to explore how the international financial system makes certain expectations of how individuals should and could act in relation to their own personal affairs, leading to processes of financial subjectification such that certain types of individual financial practices are valued more highly than others by financial services providers (French and Kneale, 2009; Langley, 2008; Marron, 2007). In particular, this approach follows wider Foucauldian work on neoliberalisation (Larner, 2007; Larner and Walters, 2005). Neoliberalisation has become widely used across the social sciences, although this has led to some concerns about the coherence and commonality, or lack thereof, in terms of the ways in which it is being used. However, for the purposes of our arguments here, the central point about neoliberalisation is that it identifies a particular form of state power that is characterised by a changing relationship between individuals and the state, within this relationship, broadly understood, individuals become increasingly personally responsible for their own economic and financial futures, rather than relying on state provision, notably through the welfare state (MacLeavy, 2008). In order for this form of state power to operate, however, it is crucial that micro-level individual economic and financial practices and decision making are controlled and managed to 'fit' within the wider national and international political and economic agenda. As such, 'programmes of neo-liberal rule unfold by seeking to secure synergies between their objectives and the motivations ... of individuals' (Barnett et al., 2008: 625).

Within this broad approach, in terms of money and finance, the use of financial products and services by individuals is seen as a form of what Foucault terms a 'technology of the self', in which particular types of financial practices and decision making are valued by politicians and policy makers within advanced economies as they seek to encourage individuals to rely on their own personal financial decision making and strategising, rather than relying on the state to support them. This is evident in the UK where, under conditions of austerity following the 2007–2008 financial crisis and ensuing recession, governments have sought aggressively to cut expenditure on social support and the welfare state (MacLeavy, 2011). For example, radical changes to the funding of higher education have reduced state financial support for university students in the UK. As a result, students are positioned as responsible consumers of finanicalised education by taking out a student loan, rather than relying on state support to facilitate their higher education. By taking out this loan finance, students are already tied into the international financial system on graduation through their debt and associated loan obligations.

Through financial products such as student fees, mortgage finance and private pension plans, a series of politically desirable (from the point of view of many governments and large financial institutions) financial subjects are created with which individuals are expected to conform. These financial subjects are assembled to embody qualities of financial responsibility, rationality and risk calculation. Taken together, these financial subject positions have been identified as representing a change such that it is no longer sufficient for individuals to act as 'passive savers', relying on relatively straightforward savings accounts coupled with the welfare state to secure their financial and economic futures. Rather, individuals are increasingly being encouraged to act as 'active investors' in which the use of debt products is increasingly deemed to be the responsible way of operating within the contemporary financial system (Langley, 2008). As a result, it is increasingly seen as irresponsible for individuals to rely on state support across the life course within neoliberalised economies; this is evidenced by the more widespread used of terms such as 'welfare scroungers' within the contemporary UK media, as the government seeks to curb what it views as a welfare dependency culture. However, research has demonstrated that there is no guarantee that individuals will act in the ways in which neoliberal governments hope and expect in terms of securing their own financial futures, and it is these contradictions and complexities that form the focus of the next section of this chapter, not least because relying on the international financial system for future

TABLE 7.1 TYPES OF FINANCIAL ADVISORS IN SINGAPORE

Characteristics	Relationship managers (RMs)	Insurance agents (IAs)	Independent financial advisors (IFAs)
Employment status	Employees of commercial banks	Self-employed, affiliated with insurance companies	Self-employed, affiliated with IFA firms
Types of financial products	In-house and some licensed products	In-house products only	No in-house products; a range of licensed products across different providers
Remunerations structures	Base salary + commission	Commission + structured incentive scheme	Commission + variable incentives
Clientele/business acquisition	Banking customers, walk-ins, branch locations, cold calling	'Warm' leads, cold calling, road shows	'Warm' leads, referrals
Administrative support (for training, compliance etc.)	Comprehensive organisational support	Comprehensive organisational support	Variables, depending on IFA firm
Branding and reputation	Brand name and reputation of bank, existing relationships	Long history of insurance companies and brand name	Least well-known; often seen as niche provider

Source: Lai (2016)

Republished with permission of John Wiley & Sons Inc, from 'Financial advisors, financial ecologies and the variegated financialisation of everyday investors', Lai, K.P.Y. *Transactions of the Institute of British Geographers*, 41 (2016); permission conveyed through Copyright Clearance Center, Inc.

household and individual financial planning is inherently risky and uncertain, given the instability of the international financial system.

Indeed, recent research has argued that the relationship between the state and individuals is increasingly mediated through a series of intermediaries, of which financial advisors have been identified as being particularly important (Lai, 2016). A range of such advisors operating in the case of Singapore are shown in Table 7.1. A key insight from this work is that such advisors are important in shaping the knowledge held by investors, and that this in turn leads to variegated investment decision making.

VARIEGATED 'INVESTOR SUBJECTS' WITHIN THE INTERNATIONAL FINANCIAL SYSTEM

Building on this identification of the variegation in the nature of 'everyday' financial subjects, a significant and politically important set of insights has been developed that moves beyond the universal globally homogenous language used by politicians in several advanced economies in the Global North. These politicians typically focus on advancing what they view as enhanced forms of financial citizenship in which individuals engage with the international financial system in appropriate ways in order to secure their own financial futures. However, a focus on the specificities of financial subjects reveals that the experiences that individuals have of acting as 'investor subjects' is variegated along a number of socio-economic lines, including age, gender, class and geography. The discussion below examines this through the cases of two types of financial products that are central to an individual's engagement with the international financial system: first, personal pension planning; and, second, life insurance.

VARIEGATED PENSION PLANNING IN FINANCIAL MARKETS IN THE UK

It is widely acknowledged that the UK pension system, in common with those of several other advanced economies, has undergone significant reform in recent years (Clark et al., 2012). In particular, in many corporate pension schemes, a defined benefit approach in which an individual and their employer made contributions and then the individual could expect a predictable income, usually based on a fraction of their final salary on retirement, has been replaced by defined contribution schemes in which the expected levels of contributions by individuals are set out, but the pension itself is dependent on how these investments perform within the international financial system. Indeed, several public pension schemes have sought to reduce their pension costs and liabilities by closing their final-salary-defined benefit schemes to new members, and replacing them either with a usually less generous defined benefit scheme linked to career-average earnings (rather than final salary), or with a defined contribution scheme.

As a result, individuals are increasingly being required to operate as responsible 'financialised subjects' (French and Kneale, 2012) in which they make decisions about how to use the financial markets as a way of guaranteeing their financial future through a private pension in order to 'top up' their state pension. A key 'market device' (Muniesa et al., 2007) within this increasingly privatised form of pension provision is the annuity. An annuity 'allows for the transformation of a lump sum on retirements (the pensions pot accrued during working life) into a set of regular (usually monthly) pension payments until the death of the annuitant' (French and Kneale, 2012: 394). What is of particular interest within this sector of the pension sector for the purposes of our arguments here are the ways in which a market for annuities has developed following 'the invention of enhanced and impaired annuities, products designed to offer better pension rates to retirees whose health, and thus life expectancy, is considered by an insurer to be "impaired"', as shown in Figure 7.1 (French and Kneale, 2012: 392). This has given rise to a range of specialised financial products such as the so-called 'smokers' pension', launched in 1995, that offers better annuity rates to smokers because of their expected shorter life expectancy and hence lower 'costs' to an annuity than their non-smoking counterparts. This has subsequently been expanded to a range of other health concerns, such as individuals deemed as being overweight and those with high blood pressure. This is an example of the often contradictory nature of the financialisation of everyday life because, while much of the neoliberal rhetoric about being a responsible financial subject centres on acting in responsible ways such as maintaining good health, these products appear to place greater value on what would often be seen as irresponsible subjects who, for example, smoke and consume alcohol. Indeed, these contradictions are further played out through what have become known as 'postcode pensions' in

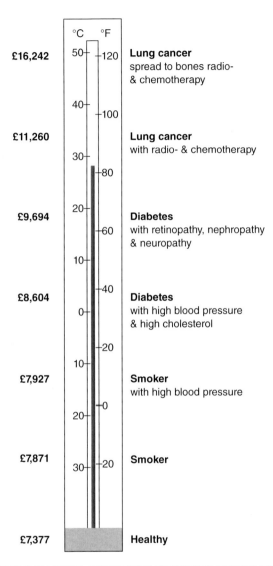

FIGURE 7.1 STYLISED EXAMPLE OF A TYPICAL ADVERTISEMENT FOR ENHANCED ANNUITIES ILLUSTRATING THE DIFFERENT RATES OF RETURN THAT CAN BE EXPECTED FROM THE SAME-SIZE PENSION POT (£100,000) FOR DIFFERENT IMPAIRMENTS, AND IN COMPARISON TO A CONVENTIONAL (HEALTHY) ANNUITY

Source: French and Kneale (2012) Reprinted with permission from Taylor & Francis. Permission conveyed through Copyright Clearance Centre, Inc.

which geo-demographics are used to offer more favourable annuity rates to individuals living in areas associated with lower life expectancy, reflecting the fact that such individuals are likely to have a shorter life expectancy. Given the ways in which these products sit at the intersection between the nature of life itself and processes of financialisation associated with individuals taking more responsibility for their financial futures, they are identified as a form of bio-financialisation (French and Kneale, 2012).

This is politically significant since it reveals how those who are, on the face of it, acting as responsible financial subjects, namely those individuals who are seeking to maintain their own health, are facing less favourable annuity rates in their pensions and hence are having to pay even greater attention to the ways in which they plan and strategise about their own financial futures.

VARIEGATED LIFE INSURANCE IN FINANCIAL MARKETS IN THE UK

The life insurance industry provides the second example of the ways in which the contradictions associated with the calling forth of particular financial subjects. While the health of individuals has been widely used in pricing the risk associated with different individuals in terms of their life insurance, more recent work has examined the

> growing attention toward and explicit mobilisation of the habits, behaviours, and lifestyles of financial subjects by insurers, not simply as proxies of mortality or morbidity risk, but increasingly as a means by which insurers seek to intervene in new ways in the everyday lives of the insured through the promulgation of active insurantial subjects. (French and Kneale, 2009: 1031)

Most notably, this industry is increasingly calling forth particular subjectivities by seeking information on the health behaviours and more general lifestyles of customers including, for example, their drinking and exercise habits. One of the earliest such initiatives was by the insurance company Swiss Re, which began to adjust premiums based on the body mass index of its customers. This was developed further in the UK by the insurance company Prudential when it founded the company PruHealth. This company identifies a number of what it deems to be health behaviours, such as restricting drinking, buying fresh fruit and vegetables from particular supermarkets and swiping in to attend gyms. When customers undertake these activities they are awarded vitality points. The accumulation of such points leads to reductions in premiums for life insurance products (see Table 7.2).

Two implications from this research are particularly important. First, it signals how the insurance and broader financial services industry is not simply responding to and creating financial products for already existing types of financial subjects, but is seeking to call forth particular forms of financial subjects by inculcating them into particular ways of acting that are deemed healthy and can be used to adjust insurance premiums. Second, this process is highly geographical because so-called health behaviours themselves, in common with life expectancy itself, vary across space. Indeed, geo-demographics can be used as a proxy measure for the key variables that are often used by the insurance industry in this respect, such as the number of units of alcohol consumed per week and the proportion of residents classified as obese through their body mass index (French and Kneale, 2009).

Given that particular types of financial subjects are rewarded, albeit in contradictory ways by the international financial system, it follows that an individual's

TABLE 7.2 EXTRACT FROM PRUHEALTH'S VITALITY POINTS TABLE

Vitality activity	Eligibility	Points per event	Maximum activity frequency	Where to earn these points	What you have to do
Exercise					
Improving fitness routine over 6-month period	All adults	300 points per vitality level improved	Once every 6 months	Vitality fitness assessments	Fax your results from the PruHealth provider to us within 45 days of the event
Organised fitness event (1 star)	All adults	50 points per event	10 per year	www.ActiveEurope.com/vitality	Register with Active Europe, click on 'claim your points' online
Purchasing eligible sporting goods from eBay	All adults	40 points per eligible item purchased	3 per year for individuals, 6 per year for families	www.eBay.co.uk	Register your eBay user ID on the Boots Health Insurance Member Zone
Not smoking					
Complete nonsmoker's declaration	All adults	150 points per year declaration made	1 per year	Declaration or through Boots Health	Visit the member zone to make declarations
Quit smoking with Allen Carr	Adult smokers	150 points	1 per policy lifetime	Check Allen Carr clinics	Points will be added automatically
Screening					
Improving blood pressure over 6-month period	All adults	100 points per vitality level improved	Once per year or more frequently as advised by your doctor	Participating fitness assessments and screening providers	Call us giving details of activity, date and medical practitioner's name and contact details
Cholesterol check (to be taken with a Boots health check)	Adult >35 years	150 points in each of the 3 years	Once every 3 years	Boots pharmacy or one of the screening providers	Visit a Boots pharmacy for your check; points will be added automatically
Nutrition					
Improving target BMI band over 6-month period	All adults	100 points per vitality level improved	Once every 6 months	Participating fitness assessments and screening providers	Fax your results from the PruHealth provider to us within 45 days of the event
Improving body fat target over 6-month period	All adults	100 points per vitality level improved	10 points for individuals per week	As above	As above
Buying fresh fruit and vegetables at Sainsbury's	All adults	1 point for every £2 spent	20 points for families per week	Shop at Sainsbury's (a national supermarket chain in the UK) online or at your local store.	Register your Nectar card (a consumer loyalty card scheme in the UK) on the Boots Health Insurance Member Zone
Education					
Complete personal health review	All adults	100 points per year	1 per year	Member Zone	Visit the Member Zone and complete the review

Source: adapted from www.pruhealth.co.uk in French and Kneale (2009)

experience of the financialisation of everyday life and their own intersection with the international financial system is likely to be very unique. In order to consider the implications of this for households and individuals, the literature on financial exclusion is particularly useful.

FINANCIAL EXCLUSION AND THE EVERYDAY LIFE OF FINANCIALISATION

The study of retail financial services is not a new area of research concern within the social sciences and economic geography in particular. For example, research on issues such as mortgage finance, negative equity and financial exclusion in the 1990s was important in the early development of the subfield of financial geography (Leyshon, 1998). These research topics have resurfaced in the 2000s, fuelled at least in part by the ways in which personal finance was so deeply implicated with the financial crisis, most notably through the central role played by mortgage finance in initially triggering the 2007–2008 crisis (see Chapter 4). That is, sub-prime (higher-risk) borrowers in certain parts of the USA (particularly the South) struggled to meet their mortgage payments following interest rate rises immediately prior to the crisis, raising questions about the potential mis-selling and use of teaser mortgage rates. These teaser rates meant that households were initially offered a very attractive interest rate which subsequently increased, often many times beyond their afford-ability, thereby meaning that borrowers defaulted on their mortgage finance. As a result, lenders in the USA became exposed to significant potential losses as they became increasingly aware that these loans might not be paid back. Personal finance has also been significantly affected following the crisis. For example, stock market falls and unpredictability as well as low interest rates have impacted negatively on pension fund performance, and access to home loans remains highly restricted in several advanced economies. While the initial interest in personal finance within economic geography and related social sciences was characterised by a political economy approach (Dymski and Veitch, 1996), recent research has adopted a more socially and culturally sensitive mode of analysis that echoes the wider development of cultural economy approaches to money and finance that underpin the approach taken in this book. In this respect, research has focused on questions of financial inclusion, exclusion and their uneven geographies.

THE GEOGRAPHIES OF FINANCIAL EXCLUSION

Financial exclusion can be understood as 'those processes by which individuals and households face difficulties in accessing financial services' (Leyshon et al., 2008: 447). Figures do not exist for the number of people who are financially excluded at any one time, partly because financial exclusion can be measured in a number of different ways. However, research shows that in 2012–2013, 1.5 million people in the UK were 'unbanked', meaning that they did not have a current bank account in their own name (Rowlingson and McKay, 2015). Nonetheless, data on how these accounts are used, which is vital if we are to understand fully the extent of financial exclusion, is not available in the public domain. That said, financial exclusion raises a number of issues:

> in an increasingly cashless society, life is difficult without access to a bank (or building society) account. For those on modest incomes and with limited savings, the risk of becoming overdrawn and incurring high charges is a powerful disincentive to operating such an account. Consumers without bank accounts may have to pay to have their wages cashed, and they may pay more for services such as gas and electricity. Those without bank accounts lose access to the wide range of services where the bank account acts as a gateway. Access to short-term credit is an important part of managing on a very restricted budget. However, people without a financial history, with inadequate savings, or problems in their credit record, can find it difficult if not impossible to obtain credit from mainstream lenders. Vulnerable consumers are likely to lack household contents insurance and be less able to replace things lost. (Marshall, 2004: 242)

CAUSES OF FINANCIAL EXCLUSION

Two related processes have been identified as exacerbating financial exclusion in recent years. First, neoliberalisation has given rise to several rounds of regulatory reform in financial services provision, allowing financial services firms to develop new financial products (targeted at particularly profitable individuals) that respond to the ways in which responsibility for socio-economic security has increasingly been transferred from the state to individuals and households. This has given rise to greater emphasis being placed on financial subjects acting as responsible individuals who, through suitable education associated with financial literacy programmes, are capable of taking and managing risks in order to manage their own financial futures (Langley, 2008). Second, technological innovation and the development of new financial products, notably those associated with securitisation, have led to a number of new channels for financial services delivery being developed and circulated transnationally that increasingly use virtual forms of communication (Leyshon and Pollard, 2000). Moreover, face-to-face risk assessment of creditworthiness, often held in branches, has increasingly been replaced by credit-scoring technologies undertaken remotely (French and Leyshon, 2004; Leyshon and Thrift, 1997; Marron, 2007). This means that an individual's credit record in terms of the amounts borrowed, the credit providers (including credit cards, mobile phone contracts as well as mortgage finance), the amount of credit outstanding and the borrower's payment history all become important factors in determining both whether credit is granted and the terms of the loan. Individuals perceived as being higher risk through poorer credit ratings, showing defaults on previous repayments for example, are therefore offered higher interest rates and potentially have their access to credit restricted altogether.

The consequences of such developments have been explored through two main areas of research that address centrally questions of space and place. First, research has

TABLE 7.3 BRANCH NETWORKS OF TOP 10 BUILDING SOCIETIES, TOP SIX BANK GROUPS AND TOP 10 CONVERTED BUILDING SOCIETIES, GREAT BRITAIN, 1989-2003

	Branches			Change (%)		
	1989	1995	2003	1989–1995	1995–2003	1989–2003
Top 10 building societies	1,699	1,478	1,403	−13.0	−5.1	−17.42
Top 6 bank groups	12,659	10,406	8,077	−17.8	−22.4	−36.2
Top 10 converted building societies	3,473	3,348	2,702	−3.6	−19.3	−22.2

Note that the figures for converted building societies include branches also included as part of the larger banking groups of which they are a part: thus, Cheltenham & Gloucester are owned by Lloyds-TSB, Halifax and Birmingham Midshires are owned by HBOS, and Woolwich Equitable is owned by Barclays

Source: French et al. (2008). Reprinted with permission of John Wiley & Sons Inc. Permission conveyed through Copyright Clearance Center, Inc.

examined the geographies of financial services withdrawal, most notably in terms of bank and building society closures from the mid-1990s onwards (see Table 7.3). This work argues that the shrinking of such branch networks by about one-third since 1989 in the UK is an important material manifestation of financial exclusion (French et al., 2008; Leyshon et al., 2008; Marshall, 2004; Marshall et al., 2000). Of particular note for my arguments here is recent work that has sought to demonstrate explicitly the importance of space and place to such processes.

This has been achieved by conceptualising the physical infrastructure of bank and building society branches as networks, the scope and density of which can be measured both by region, but also, and more significantly, along socio-economic lines. By adopting the latter approach, Leyshon et al. (2008) have demonstrated the disproportionate impact of service withdrawal in socio-economically deprived wards in the UK. As they go on to argue, the way in which financial service providers use geo-demographic data to identify where profitable financial subjects live has been a key driver of this process. As a result, financial services withdrawal in the form of bank and building society branch closures in the UK has been greater in less wealthy, more ethnically diverse parts of the country (see Table 7.4).

This focus on the geographies of processes of financial exclusion has been developed further through the identification of different forms of retail financial ecologies (Leyshon et al., 2004; 2006). This metaphor has been employed to demonstrate how the working practices of financial service providers, particularly in terms of their assessment of potential customers 'at a distance' using a range of credit-scoring techniques, is co-constitutive of financial landscapes. Leyshon et al. (2004) demonstrate the utility of this approach through the identification of two idealised types of ecology: first, the middle-class ecology in which highly financially literate subjects use a range of distribution channels to access financial services; and, second, 'relic' ecologies in which socio-economically deprived financial subjects suffer both the demise of mainstream financial provision on the basis of their lack of profitability and are instead subjected to a range of more exploitative forms of financial provision such as credit offered by door-to-door lenders.

TABLE 7.4   BRANCH CLOSURES AND OPENINGS BY BANKS, CONVERTED BUILDING SOCIETIES AND BUILDING SOCIETIES BY 'SUPERGROUP' AREA, GREAT BRITAIN, 1995-2003

'Supergroup'	Share of population 2001	Total branches 1995	Net change 1995–2003	Net change (%)	Share of branches 1995	Share of branches 2003
Industrial hinterlands	19.6	1,873	−349	−18.6	12.6	12.8
Traditional manufacturing	11.7	1,677	−374	−22.3	11.3	11.0
Built-up areas	3.3	1,832	−408	−22.3	−12.3	12.0
Prospering metropolitan	3.7	1,431	−321	−22.4	−9.6	9.4
Student communities	5.0	1,829	−387	−21.2	−12.3	12.1
Multicultural metropolitan	6.7	1,040	−245	−23.6	−7.0	6.7
Suburbs and small towns	27.7	2,651	−448	−16.9	−17.9	18.6
Coastal and countryside	17.3	2,341	−399	−17.0	−15.8	16.4
Accessible countryside	5.1	164	−36	−22.0	−1.1	1.1
Total	100	14,838	−2967	−20.0	−100	100

Source: Leyshon et al, (2008) Financial exclusion and the geography of bank and building society branch closure in Britain. *Transactions of the Institute of British Geographers,* 33(4): 447–465. Republished with permission of John Wiley & Sons Inc. Permission conveyed through Copyright Clearance Center, Inc.

Note: This analysis includes 97.5 per cent of total branches open in 1995, and 93 per cent of opening between 1995 and 2003. Branches which could not be geocoded, that is, given a location, were excluded from the analysis.

FROM FINANCIAL EXCLUSION TO REDLINING AND SUB-PRIME FINANCE

While research into retail finance provision in the UK has focused on financial inclusion and exclusion in recent years, there is a longer-standing literature that examines how financial exclusion manifests itself in the US context through work on redlining (Wyly et al., 2006; 2007; 2009). Redlining has a long history in the USA and can be dated back to at least the 1930s when the Home Owners' Loan Corporation (HOLC) was created to make loans for housing with the aim of preventing foreclosures (that is, when a mortgage lender takes ownership of a property following the borrower not making repayments as agreed). The HOLC graded neighbourhoods into four categories associated with their perceived credit risk. The fourth category was seen as the most risk and was coloured red on neighbourhood maps, giving rise to the term redlining. Crucially, such neighbourhood classification was and remains highly racialised, with black neighbourhoods dominating redlined areas.

More recently, from the 1990s onwards the US mortgage market was revolutionised. In part this stemmed from campaigns against redlining. However, it was also a function of the growth of a secondary mortgage market in which mortgage debts and their associated risks could be pooled together and bought and sold, often through securities as discussed in Chapter 4. Moreover, in a similar way to the UK, individual credit risk increasingly became assessed in more automated ways through the growth of credit reports. As a result, borrowing became easier for both wealthy and lower-income consumers. A distinctive feature of this change in the US mortgage markets was the growth in lending to low-income individuals who had historically found access to credit much more difficult. These so-called sub-prime borrowers were typically enticed into taking out credit through attractive low-interest teaser rates, but, as discussed in Chapter 5, when these expired they experienced severe difficulties in making repayments – developments that were at the heart of the 2007–2008 financial crisis. This has given rise to important debates about the extent to which the selling of such financial products amounts to 'predatory lending', in which lenders have discriminated against certain sub-prime borrowers based on their credit history by mis-selling them complex financial products which ultimately have very different terms and conditions, including interest rates, when compared with those offered to prime borrowers. Indeed, in many ways sub-prime lending represents the most recent form of redlining because:

> Subprime credit has pronounced racial and ethnic dimensions, with the highest market shares among racially marginalized *individuals* as well as predominantly minority *neighbourhoods*. (Wyly et al., 2006: 107, italics in original)

For example, Figures 7.2 and 7.3 demonstrate the highly geographically uneven concentration of sub-prime mortgage lending in the Washington–Baltimore region

FIGURE 7.2   WASHINGTON-BALTIMORE REGION

Source: Wyly et al. (2006)

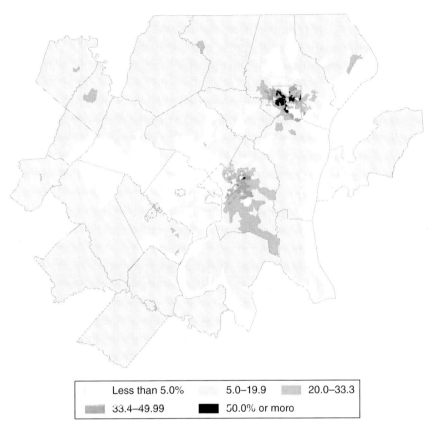

FIGURE 7.3 SUB-PRIME MARKET PENETRATION IN WASHINGTON-BALTIMORE REGION. CONVENTION REFINANCE LOANS BY SUB-PRIME LENDERS, AS A SHARE OF ALL CONVENTIONAL REFINANCE LOANS, 1998-2002

Source: Wyly et al. (2006)

in the USA. Such lending is concentrated in the city of Baltimore and areas for the east of Washington, DC, areas that have significant numbers of minority and low-income households (Wyly et al., 2006).

CONCLUSIONS

This chapter has focused on the ways in which individuals are tied into the international financial system in the wake of the 2007–2008 financial crisis. Through a focus on these everyday financial practices, the arguments presented play a potentially important role in decentring studies of financial subjects beyond a focus on financial elites as part of wider efforts to reveal the links between finance and economic processes. In particular, the chapter has demonstrated how the engagement of individuals with the international financial system is highly variegated, both by geographical region and by the socio-economic status of individuals themselves.

This analysis opens up a number of important future research agendas for cultural economy research on money and finance. First, it demonstrates the need to trace the networks of global finance beyond their production in the heartlands of the international financial system within IFCs to their consumption by individuals and households. Second, these understandings can also be used to address concerns that the spatial imaginations at work in understanding financialisation remain focused at the nation scale by revealing the importance of attending to regional and local inequalities. In so doing, the chapter contributes to the wider aims of this book by advancing cultural economy approaches to global finance through a greater attention to the places, spaces and people through which it is (re)produced.

KEY FURTHER READINGS

Aalbers, M. (2009) The financialization of home and the mortgage market crisis. *Competition and Change*, 12(2): 148–166. doi:10.1179/102452908X289802.
This paper examines the relationship between homes, the 2007 mortgage crisis and financialisation.

Lai, K.P.Y. (2016) Financial advisors, financial ecologies and the variegated financialisation of everyday investors. *Transactions of the Institute of British Geographers*, 41: 27–40.
This paper provides details of the variegated nature of 'everyday investors' and the role of financial advisors in shaping this in Singapore.

Leyshon, A., Burton, D., Knights, D., Alferoff, C. and Signoretta, P. (2004) Towards an ecology of retail financial services: understanding the persistence of door-to-door credit and insurance providers. *Environment and Planning A*, 36(4): 625–645.
This paper provides a detailed account of the different geographies of access to finance experienced in different communities in the UK.

8

AFTERWORD:
PLACING GLOBAL FINANCE

Chapter summary

- Towards a sympathetic critique of the cultural economies of global finance
- Global financial futures
    - *Digital money and finance*
    - *Crowdfunding in the UK*
    - *Finance and the environment*
- For cultural economies of finance

TOWARDS A SYMPATHETIC CRITIQUE OF THE CULTURAL ECONOMIES OF GLOBAL FINANCE

As the discussion in the previous chapters of this book demonstrate, understandings of money and finance have been developed from a number of different theoretical standpoints. In many ways, this reflects the variety of financial functions, institutions and the myriad ways in which finance is wrapped up in our daily economic lives. For example, in the run-up to the 2007–2008 financial crisis, across many social science disciplines, political economy approaches to money and finance dominated. This is, in itself, a diverse body of work, with some scholars focusing on central questions of political economy surrounding value creation and accumulation (Harvey, 1982). Meanwhile, another branch of political economy research focused upon the role of states and their regulatory arrangements in shaping the 'politics' of the financial system. This work has been particularly important in revealing how the changing governance arrangements surrounding the making and breaking of the Bretton Woods Agreement were central in creating the contemporary international financial system, as discussed in Chapter 1 (Leyshon and Thrift, 1997). Taken together, this diverse political economy literature marks a significant intervention into understandings of global finance by placing the monetary and financial system closer to the heart of the analysis of the economy than in many social science disciplines, bringing with it a recognition that money and finance had to be studied if rigorous understandings of the changing nature of the global economy were to be developed (Leyshon, 1995). This can be seen in the role played by firm finances in shaping corporate strategy and decision making (as discussed in Chapter 4) as well as the ways in which individuals' economic futures are increasingly shaped by the financial system (see Chapters 4 and 7).

However, although this political economy literature has been vital in initially positioning money and finance as a vital area of research within heterodox social science approaches to the economy, the 1990s saw a diversification in theoretical approaches and, to a lesser extent, research sites and projects. In particular, there was a growing concern to understand the social and cultural relations that underpin monetary and financial practice, in addition to the political relations that had been prioritised in earlier work (Hall, 2011). This reflects the wider interest in cultural dimensions of the economy more generally across the social sciences that developed from the 1990s onwards (for a fuller discussion of the implications of a growing interest in the cultural relations within economic life, see Amin and Thrift, 2003). In terms of work on money and finance, this development was reflected in a growing interest in the micro-foundations of finance, including the labour market practices of financial elites, the technological make-up of financial markets and the ways in which the scripting of key aspects of the financial system such as credit and debt are central to the operation of financial markets (on which see, respectively, De Goede, 2005; MacKenzie, 2006; McDowell, 1997).

It is within this dynamic and diverse intellectual landscape that this book needs to be situated. At one level, I have sought to document how this growing interest in the cultural and social dimensions of finance have crystallised through the emergence of a cultural economy approach to money and finance. As shown throughout the book, this literature has made significant interventions in advancing understandings of what is often assumed to be an 'international' or 'global' financial system. This has been achieved by revealing the ways in which global finance is produced through local sites and financial practices involving a range of components, including not only the regulatory framing and governance of financial markets as emphasised by earlier political research, but also the materiality of financial markets, such as computer trading screens, individual working practice and the scripting of finance in particular ways. In so doing, cultural economy approaches to money and finance have done much to reveal the ongoing 'work' required to create, reproduce and develop financial markets.

However, the analysis in this book is also intended to demonstrate that, as the cultural economy literature has matured over at least the last 15 years, it is also important and timely to develop a sympathetic critique of its contribution. Two main avenues of such a critique have been developed. First, it is important to situate the sites used to produce cultural economy research and recognise its largely partial account of what is often labelled as 'global' finance to date. In this respect, and partly reflecting its development during the financial boom of the 2000s, cultural economy research has focused its research activities on IFCs in Europe and North America (although, for a notable exception, see Hertz, 1998; Knorr Cetina and Bruegger, 2002). As a result, while detailed understandings of the transformation of these financial markets have been developed, for example through the rise of screen-based financial trading (Zaloom, 2006), less is known about how the making of financial markets varies across space and the ways in which distant geographical relations between financial centres are important in the constitution of the financial system. In response, this book has sought to extend cultural economy analysis beyond the heartlands of its own knowledge production and pay greater attention to locations and financial practices emanating from beyond Europe and North America in the making of financial markets. Particular attention in this respect has been paid to the changing geographies of finance within China and Asia, as financial centres here, including Singapore, Beijing and Shanghai, increasingly play an important role in shaping the international financial system.

However, the importance of attending to these more diverse spatialities is not limited to simply diversifying the site of knowledge production within cultural economy or documenting the variegation of financial markets to demonstrate that financial markets operate in different ways in different places. The second element of the sympathetic critique developed within this book argues that while taking the geographical specificity of financial making seriously, it is important not to jettison the political and critical approach to money and finance developed within earlier political economy research within a cultural economy tradition. In this respect, although cultural economy research has carefully identified a number of important elements that are combined in the making of financial markets, it has been argued in this book that this approach serves to glamorise the world of high finance. In particular, it is argued that by focusing on the complexity of financial markets, this complexity has been used as a veil with which to shield financial markets from critical discussion and research. For example, Christophers has interrogated the notion of complexity within financial markets

> to unsettle two powerful but problematic dispositions. One is the tendency for commentators to use the perception (or excuse) of complexity to absolve themselves of the requirement to undertake truly meaningful analysis. The other is the inclination to blame complexity *for* crisis – to invoke 'complexity' as a *causal* and *sufficient* explanation of crisis in and of itself. (2009: 808, italics in original)

In response to this criticism, in this book I have suggested that a greater attentiveness to the ways in which financial markets are made differently in different places because of the regulatory and institutional landscape (in particular places and financial centres) provides a valuable way of developing a more critically and politically attuned cultural economy of money and finance. For example, the discussion of the internationalisation of the Chinese currency, the RMB, in Chapter 3 reveals that in order to understand how new RMB markets are made requires not just a close reading of the material constitution of these markets through their specific financial instruments, for example; it is also necessary to consider how RMB internationalisation is tied into wider geo-political concerns surrounding the changing place of China within the global economy. Indeed, the power relations between the UK and Chinese governments and their financial authorities, as well as the role of regulation, are both central in order to understand how and why London developed as the first and leading western offshore RMB centre.

Such a sensitivity to the variegated nature of money and finance has also allowed the development of critical approaches to contemporary finance in the wake of the financial crisis through documenting, for example, the uneven experiences of what is often termed the 'global financial crisis' of 2007–2008 even within what are assumed to be the heartlands of the international financial system in the USA. Here the literature on financialisation has been particularly instructive and clearly critiques any understanding of the world of high finance as being somehow either detached from our everyday economic lives or separated from other aspects of what are sometimes termed the 'real economy', such as manufacturing (Hall, 2012). This work reminds us of the ways in which global finance becomes grounded and enacted in different ways in different places, often with highly uneven outcomes.

GLOBAL FINANCIAL FUTURES

As would be expected of a dynamic research field, while this book has considered the main areas of enquiry and its limitations from a cultural economy perspective, important new avenues for future research are constantly emerging. The rest of this chapter briefly examines two of these and considers the potential they offer to continue to develop a geographically sensitive, politically attuned, cultural understanding of global finance.

DIGITAL MONEY AND FINANCE

One of the most significant developments in money and finance in the 2010s has been the so-called 'fintech' (financial technology) revolution (*The Economist*, 2015). This revolution consists of the rapid growth, particularly in the wake of the financial crisis, of financial technology start-up companies that offer a range of services including payments, wealth management, peer-to-peer lending and crowdfunding. Figures point to the rapid growth of this sector. For example, in 2014 these firms attracted $12 billion in investment, an increase of $4 billion on 2013 (*The Economist*, 2015). The ability of such firms to challenge, or disrupt, the operations of incumbent financial institutions, particularly large multinational banks, is keenly debated and, while it is in many ways too early to tell, there are signs that these technology firms will pose some significant challenges to established financial institutions that will have important implications for the ways in which financial markets are made and reproduced in the future.

First, although the amount of lending made by fintech companies remains small, their significance lies in their different business models as compared with mainstream banks. In particular, they are not trying to manage the legacy costs of extensive branch networks and older computer infrastructures, issues that we saw in Chapter 7 were already changing the nature of retail banking in several geographical markets. This means that fintech companies typically have a lower cost base than their more long-standing competitors and hence are often able to offer better rates and fee structures to their customers. Second, these fintech companies are introducing new ways of assessing risk, particularly through the use of the social media activity of their customers. The potential for this approach to credit scoring to become more mainstream alongside the established practices of credit rating agencies such as Experian and Equifax was demonstrated in the UK in November 2016 when the car insurer Admiral announced that it would analyse the Facebook accounts of first-time car owners in order to use an algorithm that uses their posts to produce a likely profile for them in terms of their driving style:

> Admiral Insurance will analyse the Facebook accounts of first-time car owners to look for personality traits that are linked to safe driving. For example, individuals who are identified as conscientious and well-organised will score well. The insurer will examine posts and likes by the Facebook user, although not photos, looking for habits that research shows are linked to these traits. These include writing in short concrete sentences, using lists, and arranging to meet friends at a set time and place, rather than just 'tonight'. (*Guardian*, 2016)

Third, fintech firms deal with leverage in a very different way to mainstream banks. Whereas the latter transform deposits into longer-term assets such as mortgage finance, in fintech lending, especially that which is peer to peer, the lender and borrower are matched through the fintech firm and the lender carries the risk of default until the borrower makes the final payment and is committed as a lender up until that point. As *The Economist* notes, while the likelihood of fintech firms becoming dominant within mainstream finance currently seems rather remote, the existence of these firms is already shaping financial market making in important ways:

> If fintech platforms were ever to become the main sources of capital for households and firms, the established industry would be transformed into something akin to 'narrow banking'. Traditional banks would take deposits and hold only safe, liquid assets, while fintech platforms matched borrowers and savers. Economies would operate with much less leverage than today. But long before then, upstarts will force banks to accept lower margins. Conventional lenders will charge more for the services that the newcomers cannot easily replicate, including the payments infrastructure and the provision of an insured current account. The bigger effect

from the fintech revolution will be to force flabby incumbents to cut costs and improve the quality of their service. That will change finance as profoundly as any regulator has. (*The Economist*, 2015)

CROWDFUNDING IN THE UK

One of the areas of fintech activity that is most well developed and has begun to attract growing academic research attention is that of crowdfunding, part of what has been termed 'platform capitalism' (Langley and Leyshon, 2016). As part of the digital economy, crowdfunding developed in the USA and UK in the late 2000s and is defined as follows:

> Rather than carrying ideas and knowledge or making car rides or rooms available, crowdfunding circuits transfer funds that are provided by large numbers of individuals who are collectively referred to as the crowd. Funds are aggregated and distributed through online platforms to a range of actors and institutions, including artists and performers, charitable and community projects, and start-up businesses and small- and medium-sized enterprises (SMEs). (Langley, 2016: 302)

By seeking to match borrowers and lenders through platforms which, beyond the case of finance, include well-known names such as Uber and Airbnb, crowdfunding does not involve the difference between short-term liabilities and longer-term assets, as typifies mainstream banking. However, within this shared approach, a diversity of crowdfunding circuits have emerged in the UK as Table 8.1 shows. Moreover, as Figure 8.1 shows, the growth of the sector in the UK has been rapid, with annual growth rates averaging 75 per cent between 2011 and 2013 (Langley, 2016) and with estimates suggesting that crowdfunding is responsible for 3 per cent of gross lending to small and medium-sized enterprises in 2015 (Langley and Leyshon, 2016).

TABLE 8.1   THE PRINCIPAL CROWDFUNDING CIRCUITS IN THE UK: A TYPOLOGY

Circuit	Typical funding recipients	Financial instruments	Leading platforms
Donation	Individuals; Community projects Registered charities Social enterprises	None	Buzzbnk, Hubbub, Indiegogo, JustGiving
Reward	Individuals Community projects Social enterprises	None	Buzzbnk, CrowdPatch, Indiegogo, Kickstarter
Fixed-income	SMEs Social enterprises	Debentures Mini-bonds	Abundance Generation, Crowdcube
Equity	Start-ups	Shares	CrowdBnk, Crowdcube, Seedrs
Peer-to-peer	Individuals SMEs	Unsecured loans	Funding Circle, RateSetter, Zopa

Source: 'Crowdfunding in the UK: a cultural economy', Langley, P. *Economic Geography* 92(3) (2016), reprinted by permission of the publisher Taylor & Francis Ltd, http://www.tandfonline.com.

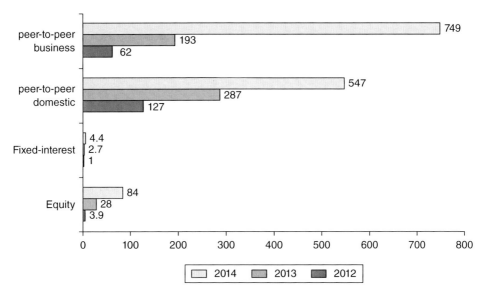

FIGURE 8.1 AGGREGATE ANNUAL FLOWS IN FINANCIAL MARKET CIRCUITS OF UK CROWDFUNDING (£M)

Source: Langley (2016) drawing on Nesta (2014)

While research in this area is still in its early stages, given the relatively recent development of crowdfunding itself, there are already some important research questions being asked and agendas being set for future research into the contemporary nature of finance. First, crowdfunding, and fintech more generally, place questions of money more centrally within understandings of broader financial circuits and systems, something that has received comparatively less attention in recent years (Langley, 2016). In particular, crowdfunding, and other monetary forms within the fintech sector, perhaps most notably bitcoin, raise fundamental questions about how trust is placed in money, how it is valued and how it is circulated as a means of exchange. Third, there is an important emerging geography to fintech itself. There is already a dynamic fintech cluster situated around Old Street on the edge of the historic City of London, colloquially known as Silicon Roundabout. How this cluster, and others like it, sit alongside the more established clusters within IFCs, the relationship between the two and the implications of this for both mainstream and technologically mediated finance will be important questions to address as fintech increasingly, and literally, intersects with the financial circuits that have been the main focus of analysis in this book.

FINANCE AND THE ENVIRONMENT

The second research area through which critically and politically attuned cultural economies are developing is at the intersection between finance and the environment. In many ways this work combines insights from both the financialisation literature discussed in detail in Chapter 4 and the broader arguments concerning cultural economy put forward in the book as a whole, because it examines how finance is becoming increasingly entangled with the environment in ways that echo the ways that the financialisation literature draws attention to the networks between finance and the so-called 'real economy'. Moreover, by focusing on the micro-practices and materiality of how such entanglements become realised, this literature also clearly draws on cultural economy insights.

Set within this theoretical landscape, work at the intersection between finance and the environment is predominately focused, albeit in a different sense, on the ways in which government and societies are increasingly interested in the ways in which anthropogenically induced climate change can be managed through financial markets (Knox-Hayes, 2013). By interrogating the ways in which these new forms of financial markets might be developed in this way, this work sounds a note of caution about the extent to which markets can be used to address climate change. Indeed, one of the biggest issues of such endeavours is the work needed to transform elements of the environment, such as carbon reduction, water and fish, into a tradable commodity which involves a considerable amount of scientific expertise and institutional and political support (on which see, respectively, Bumpus and Liverman, 2008; Bakker, 2005; Mansfield, 2004).

One of the financial markets related to environmental change that has been considered most fully is the market involved in the trading of carbon, and carbon offsets in particular:

> The concept of offsets emerged in the Kyoto Protocol's flexible mechanisms (UN Framework Convention on Climate Change, UNFCCC 1997), which allow industrialised countries to meet their emission-reduction targets by purchasing emission reductions that are associated with projects in the developing world (the Clean Development Mechanism, CDM) or eastern European economies in transition (Joint Implementation). Together with carbon trading, these mechanisms provide an alternative to more expensive or politically difficult domestic emission reductions. (Bumpus and Liverman, 2008: 128)

One of the most significant market responses to the development of offsets is the EU Emissions Trading System (EU ETS), launched in 2005. This system is based on 'cap and trade' principles in which power and industrial installations have capped levels of carbon emissions and any variation (higher or lower than the cap) can be sold on and subsequently traded in order to meet the overall aim of reducing emissions. The existence of this market has drawn heavily on the financial architecture of the EU, and London's financial district in particular, in order to create physically a market for the trade of these carbon offsets. The fact that these markets have been created relatively recently through a distinctive set of policy interventions provides an important opportunity to examine the challenges of creating new forms of financial markets (Knox-Hayes, 2009).

Research into the creation of these new financial markets documents how, in many ways, they echo the existing financial infrastructure of the international financial system, with the financial districts of London and New York serving as the most significant trading centres (Knox-Hayes, 2009). For example, the creation of financial products related to carbon trading involves a significant amount of legal and accountancy work, and research has shown how the expertise developed in existing financial markets in leading IFCs within corporate law firms has been central in creating such products. Moreover, these IFCs can also provide the market liquidity needed to support carbon markets through the clusters of brokers, banks and exchanges that they house. However, while some forms of expertise have been drawn on to support the development of these markets, other forms of financial expertise are challenged by the creation of these markets. For example, a number of questions have been raised about the accountancy implications of carbon markets, particularly the need to harmonise accountancy standards in this area so that information about participating companies can be compared (Lovell et al., 2013).

The challenges of converting elements of the environment into financial products that can be traded in IFCs are also found in the rise of new insurance products related to severe disasters such as tsunamis and earthquakes, as well as pandemic health crises such as flu pandemics, in which these events have to be framed as risks that can be priced and circulated as financial instruments. These financial products are termed 'insurance-linked securities' (ILS) and are

> typically bonds, swaps, and futures whose rate of return depends on whether or not a pre-specified insurance loss trigger occurs within a certain time period. (Johnson, 2013)

Catastrophe bonds are the most well-known such financial products. These are designed to

> move especially concentrated geographic exposures from an insurer's or reinsurer's portfolio outward into the broader financial markets. … If a bond is 'triggered' by a catastrophic event, investors lose part or all their principal. If not, they collect quarterly payments as well as a return of their principal at the bond's maturation date. (Johnson, 2014: 157)

The most common events transformed into these financial products are natural catastrophes that impact upon insurable materialities such as houses and infrastructure, including earthquakes and hurricanes. Other bonds are linked to events in a particular geographical location, for example an earthquake in a particular US city region. Work in this vein is critically engaging with the challenges posed by developing new financial markets linked to significant ecological change and events, and therefore marks an important intervention in calls for research on money and finance to explore the ways in which financial logics and illogics are co-constitutive of other realms of economic life. In so doing, it focuses attention on the constant challenge faced as seemingly powerful financial logics are put to work in new areas of economic life and on the work of a range of experts and practitioners that is central to the making of these new financial markets.

FOR CULTURAL ECONOMIES OF FINANCE

Although the fintech sector and the intersection between finance and the environment represent just two important examples, in discussing them briefly here I hope to show the continued relevance, power and need to develop politically and geographically sensitive accounts of the making of financial markets in the future. This is particularly true as new forms of financial markets, their associated technologies and institutional framings are developed in the wake of significant changes in the world economy more generally. Indeed, given the election of Donald Trump as President of the United States, the vote by the UK to leave the EU in 2016 and the continued uncertainties surrounding the role played by China within the global economy, being sensitive to how place-specific institutional arrangements and their politics shape financial markets and practice will become more important then ever.

The arguments developed in this book reveal the considerable potential that a critical cultural economy of finance might make to understanding how the financial system is reproduced, and also contributes to these significant changes to the geopolitics of the world economy. By remaining attentive to how what can be viewed as a seemingly all-powerful and homogeneous international financial system is created, reproduced and challenged through a series of local practices, grounded in particular institutional and socio-cultural landscapes, a cultural economy approach is capable of revealing the variegated nature of 'global finance' and the ways in which it is assembled and contested through a series of market practices, themselves grounded in specific places and their spatial relations. Given the continued power of financial logics within economic life and the increasing challenge to many of our taken-for-granted assumptions about the organisation and politics of the global economy, documenting how finance operates in this way, from the bottom up, has a vital role to play in understanding the operations and often unequal outcomes associated with contemporary 'global finance'.

KEY FURTHER READINGS

Knox-Hayes, J. (2009) The developing carbon financial service industry: expertise, adaptation and complementarity in London and New York. *Journal of Economic Geography*, 9: 749-777.
This paper provides a detailed discussion of the relationship between carbon trading markets and established IFCs.

Langley, P. (2016) Crowdfunding in the UK: a cultural economy. *Economic Geography*, 92(3): 301-321.
This paper presents a geographical perspective of one of the first critical engagements with the rise of crowdfunding as a form of finance.

GLOSSARY

Asset-backed securities

This is a security (credit-based relationship between a borrower and a lender) backed by the cash flow from a collected pool of assets such as car loans or student loans. Mortgage-backed securities are a form of asset-backed securities in which the asset is a mortgage loan.

Bretton Woods Agreement

This agreement was made in 1944 between the USA, Canada, allied states of the US in Western Europe, Australia and Japan. It served as the foundation for the international financial system following the Second World War. It involved a system of pegged exchange rates facilitated through the US dollar being linked to the value of gold, giving rise to the term the 'gold standard'. This tightly controlled system of exchange rates was supported by multilateral organisations including the General Agreement on Tariffs and Trade (GATT), the International Bank for Reconstruction and the International Monetary Fund (IMF). The agreement collapsed in 1973 as the dollar's ability to match the price of gold came under increasing pressure.

Collateralised debt obligations

These are a form of asset-backed security in which the asset is based on a form of debt obligation such as a student loan or car loan repayment.

Credit default swaps

These are a form of insurance taken out against financial instruments such as bonds to protect against the possibility that the original financial instrument loses value.

Crowdfunding

This is a way of raising finance through contributions from a large number of people (the crowd). Internet-mediated platforms are increasingly used to manage the process.

De-territorialisation

The process by which economic practices become increasingly separative and distinct from the place of their origination.

Exchange rate

The rate at which two different national currencies are exchanged.

Financialisation

A shorthand used to describe and outline the growing power of finance within an economy.

Gentlemanly capitalism

A term used to describe the male-dominated, socially homogeneous, interpersonal networks that have been central in the development of London's international financial district, often based around the shared educational background of the network members at a small number of elite fee-paying schools and universities.

Gold standard

This refers to the period under the Bretton Woods Agreement during which the value of the US dollar was linked to gold, and other international currencies were, in turn, pegged to the dollar.

International financial centres

These are relatively small districts, often within large global cities, in which financial and related service activities (such as legal services, accountancy and management consultancy) are concentrated. They serve as important locations for the reproduction of the international financial system.

Islamic financial system

This is a banking and financial system that is sharia compliant: that is, compliant with Islamic law.

Offshore finance

Financial services activity that takes place outside of mainstream financial centres, often in places with lower levels of regulation and transparency.

Old boys' network

A term used to describe the male-dominated social networks often used to hire and secure upward progression in London's financial district.

Peer-to-peer lending

Usually mediated via an online platform such as Zopa and Ratesetter, these peer-to-peer lenders bring together lenders and borrowers without going through a mainstream bank, with the expectation that each will receive a better rate than would be available through the mainstream banking system.

Redlining

Originating in the United States, redlining involves not providing financial services, or providing them at a higher cost, to residents in particular places based on the racial and/or ethnic make-up of those places.

Reserve currency

A reserve currency is held by governments and institutions to make up their foreign exchange reserves. As such it is seen as a relatively 'safe haven'. The US dollar is usually identified as the current global reserve currency, although there is some debate as to the extent to which this could be challenged by other currencies in the future, notably the Chinese currency, the renminbi.

Securitisation

This is the process through which a series of assets are pooled and then classified or tranched (or subdivided) according to different risk profiles. These pooled assets are then sold on through products including asset-backed securities and collateralised debt obligations.

Sub-prime

Credit or loan agreements offered to individuals or firms with a poor credit r-ating history, often at higher cost.

REFERENCES

Aalbers, M. (2009a) Geographies of the financial crisis. *Area*, 41(1): 34–42.

Aalbers, M. (2009b) The financialization of home and the mortgage market crisis. *Competition and Change*, 12(2): 148–166.

Allen, J. and Pryke, M. (2013) Financializing household water: Thames Water, MEIF and 'ring fenced' politics. *Cambridge Journal of Regions, Economy and Society*, 6: 419–439.

Altman, R. (2009) 'We cannot return to the old macho ways', *The Observer* 15 February.

Amin, A. (2002) Spatialities of globalization. *Environment and Planning A*, 34: 385–399.

Amin, A. and Thrift, N. (1992) Neo-Marshallian nodes in global networks. *International Journal of Urban and Regional Research*, 16: 571–587.

Amin, A. and Thrift, N. (2003) *The Blackwell Cultural Economy Reader*. Oxford: Blackwell.

ASIFMA (2014) *RMB roadmap*. Hong Kong: ASIFMA.

Atkinson, A.B. and Piketty, T. (eds) (2010) *Top Incomes: Global Perspective*. Oxford: Oxford University Press.

Atlantic Council (2015) *Renminbi Ascending*. Washington, DC: Atlantic Council.

Augar, P. (2001) *The Death of Gentlemanly Capitalism: The Rise and Fall of London's Investment Banks*. London: Penguin.

Augar, P. (2009) *Chasing Alpha: How Reckless Growth and Unchecked Ambition Ruined the City's Golden Decade*. London: Bodley Head.

Bakk-Simon, K., Borgoli, S., Giron, C., Hempell, H., Maddaloni, A., Recine, F. and Rosati, S. (2012) Shadow banking in the Euro Area: an overview. *ECB Occasional Paper Series*, No. 133, European Central Bank. Available at: www.ecb.europa.eu/pub/pdf/scpops/ecbocp133.pdf, last accessed 14 December 2016.

Bakker, K. (2005) Neoliberalizing nature? Market environmentalism in water supply in England and Wales. *Annals of the Association of American Geographers*, 95: 542–565.

Barclay's Capital (2012) Barclay's Capital advert for 2012 Summer Analyst Program.

Barnett, C., Clarke, N., Cloke, P. and Malpass, A. (2008) The elusive subjects of neo-liberalism: beyond the analytics of governmentality. *Cultural Studies,* 22(5): 624–653

Bassens, D. (2012) Emerging markets in a shifting global financial architecture: the case of Islamic securitization in the Gulf region. *Geography Compass*, 6(6): 340–350.

Bassens, D., Derudder, B. and Witlox, F. (2010) Searching for the Mecca of finance: Islamic financial services and the world city network, *Area,* 42(1): 35-46.

Bathelt, H. and Gluckler, J. (2003) Towards a relational economic geography. *Journal of Economic Geography*, 3: 117–144.

Bathelt, H., Malmberg, A. and Maskell, P. (2004) Clusters and knowledge: local buzz, global pipelines and the process of knowledge creation. *Progress in Human Geography*, 28: 31–56.

Beaverstock, J.V. (2004) 'Managing across borders': knowledge management and expatriation in professional service legal firms. *Journal of Economic Geography*, 4(2): 157–179.

Beaverstock, J.V. (2005) Transnational elites in the city: British highly-skilled inter-company transferees in New York City's financial district. *Journal of Ethnic and Migration Studies*, 31: 245–268.

Beaverstock, J.V. (2011) Servicing British expatriate 'talent' in Singapore: exploring ordinary transnationalism and the role of the 'expatriate club'. *Journal of Ethnic and Migration Studies,* 37: 709–728.

Beaverstock, J.V and Doel, M. (2001) Unfolding the spatial architecture of the East Asian financial crisis: the orgnaizational response of global investment banks. *Geoforum* 32(1) 15–32.

Beaverstock, J.V. and Hall, S. (2012) Competing for talent: global mobility, immigration and the City of London's labour market. *Cambridge Journal of Regions, Economy and Society*, 5(2): 271–288.

Beaverstock, J.V. and Hall, S. (2016) Super-rich capitalism: managing and preserving private wealth management in the offshore world. In I. Hay and J.V. Beaverstock (eds), *Handbook of Wealth and the Super-Rich*. Cheltenham: Edward Elgar. pp. 401–421.

Beaverstock, J., Smith, R. and Taylor, P. (2000) World city network: A new meta-geography?' *Annals of the Association of American Geographers*, 90: 123–134.

Beaverstock, J.V., Doel, M.A., Hubbard, P. and Taylor, P. (2002) Attending to the world: competition, cooperation and connectivity in the world city network. *Global Networks*, 2(2): 96–116.

Beaverstock, J.V., Hall, S. and Wainwright, T. (2013a) Servicing the super-rich: new financial elites and the rise of the private wealth management retail ecology. *Regional Studies*, 47(6): 834–849.

Beaverstock, J.V., Hall, S.J.E. and Wainwright, T. (2013b) Overseeing the fortunes of the global super-rich: the nature of private wealth management in London's financial district. In I. Hay (ed.), *Geographies of the Super-Rich*. Cheltenham: Edward Elgar. pp. 43–60.

Berndt, C. and Boeckler, M. (2009) Geographies of circulation and exchange: constructions of markets. *Progress in Human Geography*, 33(4): 535–551.

BIS (2010a) Financing a private sector recovery. Department for Business, Innovation and Skills, Crown Copyright, London.

BIS (2010b) The path to strong, sustainable and balanced growth. Department for Business, Innovation and Skills, Crown Copyright, London.

BIS (2011) The plan for growth. Department for Business, Innovation and Skills, Crown Copyright, London.

Bourdieu, P. (1990) *The Logic of Practice*. Stanford, CA: Stanford University Press.

Bourdieu, P. (1996) *The State Nobility: Elite Schools in the Field of Power*. Stanford, CA: Stanford University Press.

Boussebaa, M., Morgan, G. and Sturdy, A. (2012) Constructing global firms? National, transnational and neocolonial effects in international management consultancies. *Organization Studies*, 33(4): 465–486.

Bumpus, A. and Liverman, D. (2008) Accumulation by decarbonization and the governance of carbon offsets. *Economic Geography*, 84(2): 127–155.

Burn, G. (1999) The state, the City and the Euromarkets. *Review of International Political Economy*, 6(2): 225–261.

Burton, D., Knights, D., Leyshon, A., Alferoff, C. and Signoretta, P. (2004) Making a market: the UK retail financial services industry and the rise of the complex sub-prime credit market. *Competition & Change*, 8: 3–25.

Cain, P.J. and Hopkins, A.G. (1986) Gentlemanly capitalism and British expansion overseas I. The colonial system 1688–1850. *Economic History Review*, 39(4): 501–525.

Cain, P.J. and Hopkins, A.G. (1987) Gentlemanly capitalism and British expansion overseas II. New imperialism, 1850–1945. *Economic History Review*, 40(1): 1–26.

Caliskan, K. and Callon, M. (2009) Economization, part 1: shifting attention from the economy towards processes of economization. *Economy and Society*, 38: 369–398.

Caliskan, K. and Callon, M. (2010) Economization, part 2: a research programme for the study of markets. *Economy and Society*, 39(1): 1–32.

Callon, M. (2007) What does it mean to say that economics is performative? In D. MacKenzie, F. Muniesa and L. Siu (eds), *Do Economists Make Markets? On the Performativity of Economics*. Princeton, NJ: Princeton University Press. pp. 311–57.

Castells, M. (1996) *The Rise of the Network Society*. Oxford: Blackwell.

Chen, X. and Cheung, Y.-W. (2011) Renminbi going global. *China & World Economy*, 19(2): 1–18.

Christophers, B. (2009) Complexity, finance and progress in human geography. *Progress in Human Geography*, 33: 807–824.

Christophers, B. (2011a) Making finance productive. *Economy and Society*, 40: 112–140.

Christophers, B. (2011b) Follow the thing: money. *Environment and Planning D*, 29: 1068–1084.

Christophers, B. (2011c) Credit, where credit's due. Response to 'Follow the thing: credit'. *Environment and Planning D*, 29: 1089–1091.

Christophers, B. (2015) The limits to financialization. *Dialogues in Human Geography*, 5(2): 183–200.

City of London (2015) 'The Changing Face of the City of London'. Prepared by the City of London Corporation, April 2015. Available at: https://www.cityoflondon.gov.uk/business/economic-research-and-information/research-publications/Documents/research-2015/Changing-face-of-the-City-WEB.pdf.

Claessens, S., Dell'Ariccia, G., Igan, D. and Laeven, L. (2010) Cross-country experiences and policy implications from the global financial crisis. *Economic Policy*, 25(62): 267–293.

Clark, G. (2000) *Pension Fund Capitalism*. Oxford: Oxford University Press.

Clark, G.L. (2003) *European Pensions and Global Finance*. Oxford: Oxford University Press.

Clark, G. and Monk, A. (2010a) The legitimacy and governance of Norway's sovereign wealth fund: the ethics of global investment. *Environment and Planning A*, 42: 1723–1738.

Clark, G. and Monk, A. (2010b) Government of Singapore Investment Corporation (GIC): insurer of last resort and bulwark of nation-state legitimacy. *Pacific Review*, 23: 429–451.

Clark, G. and O'Connor, K. (1997) The informational content of financial products and the spatial structure of the global finance industry. In K. Cox (ed.), *Spaces of Globalization: Reasserting the Power of the Local*. New York: Guilford. pp. 89–114.

Clark, G.L. and Wójcik, D. (2007) *The Geography of Finance: Corporate Governance in the Global Marketplace*. Oxford: Oxford University Press.

Clark, G., Monk, A., Dixon, A., Pauly, L., Faulconbridge, J., Yeung, H. and Behrendt, S. (2010) Symposium: Sovereign fund capitalism. *Environment and Planning A*, 42: 2271–2291.

Clark, G., Strauss, K. and Knox-Hayes, J. (2012) *Saving for Retirement*. Oxford: Oxford University Press.

Clark, G.L., Dixon, A.D., and Monk, A.H.B. (2013). *Sovereign Wealth Funds: Legitimacy, Governance, and Global Power*. Princeton, NJ: Princeton University Press.

Clark, G.L., Lai, K. and Wójcik, D. (2015) Editorial introduction to the special section: deconstructing offshore finance. *Economic Geography*, 91: 237–249.

Clarke, W. (2001) *How the City of London Works: An Introduction to its Financial Markets*, 5th edition. London: Sweet and Maxwell.

CMLGWM (2009) World Wealth Report 2009. Available at: https://www.capgemini.com/resource-file-access/resource/pdf/World_Wealth_Report_2009.pdf.

Cobb, S. (1998) Global finance and the growth of offshore financial centres: the Manx experience. *Geoforum*, 29: 7–21.

Cobb, S. (1999) The role of corporate, professional and personal networks in the provision of offshore financial services. *Environment and Planning A*, 31: 1877–1892.

Cobham, A., Jansky, P. and Menzer, M. (2015) The financial secrecy index: shedding new light on the geography of secrecy. *Economic Geography*, 91: 281–303.

Coe, N.M. and Wrigley, N. (2007) Host economy impacts of retail TNCs: the research agenda. *Journal of Economic Geography*, 7(4): 341–371.

Coe, N.M., Dicken, P. and Hess, M. (2008) Introduction: global production networks – debates and challenges. *Journal of Economic Geography*, 8(3): 267–269.

Coe, N.M., Lai, K. and Wójcik, D. (2014) Integrating finance into global production networks. *Regional Studies*, 48: 761–777.

Collins, M. (1991) *Banks and Industrial Finance in Britain 1800–1939*. Cambridge: Cambridge University Press.

Cook, A., Faulconbridge, J.R. and Muzio, D. (2012) London's legal elite: recruitment through cultural capital and the reproduction of social exclusivity in City professional service fields. *Environment and Planning A*, 44: 1744–1762.

Cook, G.A.S., Pandit, N.R., Beaverstock, J.V., Taylor, P.J. and Pain, K. (2007) The role of location in knowledge creation and diffusion: evidence of centripetal and centrifugal forces in the City of London financial services agglomeration. *Environment and Planning A*, 39(6): 1325–1345.

Coppock, S. (2013) The everyday geographies of financialisation: impacts, subjects and alternatives. *Cambridge Journal of Regions, Economy and Society*, 6(3): 479–500.

Crotty, J. (2008) If financial market competition is intense, why are financial firm profits so high? Reflections on the current 'golden age' of finance. *Competition and Change*, 12: 167–183.

Dawley, S., Marshall, N., Pike, A., Pollard, J. and Tomaney, J. (2014) Continuity and evolution in an old industrial region: the labour market dynamics of the rise and fall of Northern Rock. *Regional Studies*, 48(1): 154–172.

Dean, M. (1999) *Governmentality: Power and Rule in Modern Society.* London: Sage.

De Goede, M. (2005) *A Genealogy of Finance: Virtue, Fortune and Faith.* Minneapolis: University of Minnesota Press.

Deutsche Bank (2014) *At the centre of RMB internationalisation: a brief guide to offshore RMB.* Deutsche Bank AG.

Dicken, P. (2011) *Global Shift: Mapping the Contours of the Changing World Economy.* London: Sage.

Dicken, P. and Malmberg, A. (2001) Firms in territories: a relational perspective. *Economic Geography*, 77: 345–363.

Dicken, P. and Thrift, N. (1992) The organization of production and the production of organization: why business enterprises matter in the study of geographical industrialization. *Transactions of the Institute of British Geographers*, 17: 279–291.

Dicken, P., Kelly, P.F., Olds, K. and Wai-Chung Yeung, H. (2001) Chains and networks, territories and scales: towards a relational framework for analysing the global economy. *Global Networks*, 1(2): 89–112.

Dixon, A. (2011) Variegated capitalism and the geographies of finance: towards a common agenda. *Progress in Human Geography*, 35: 193–210.

Dixon, A.D. (2014) *The New Geography of Capitalism: Firms, Finance and Society.* Oxford: Oxford University Press.

Dodd, N. (1994) *The Sociology of Money: Economics, Reason and Contemporary Society.* New York: Continuum.

Dodd, N. (2014) *The Social Life of Money.* Princeton, NJ: Princeton University Press.

Dow, S. (1999) The stages of banking development and the spatial evolution of financial systems. In R. Martin (ed.), *Money and the Space Economy.* Chichester: Wiley-Blackwell. pp. 31–48.

Dymski, G.A. and Veitch, J.M. (1996) Financial transformation and the metropolis: booms, busts and banking in Los Angeles. *Environment and Planning A*, 28: 1233–1260.

The Economist (2011) Rebalancing the economy: less paper, more iron. 7 July.

The Economist (2015) The fintech revolution. 9 May.

Engelen, E. and Faulconbridge, J. (2009) Introduction: financial geographies – the credit crisis as an opportunity to catch economic geography's next boat? *Journal of Economic Geography*, 9: 587–595.

Engelen, E. and Glasmacher, A. (2013) Multiple financial modernities: international financial centres, urban boosters and the internet as the site of negotiations. *Regional Studies*, 47(6): 850–867.

Engelen, E., Erturk, I., Froud, J., Leaver, A. and Williams, K. (2010) Reconceptualising financial innovation: frame, conjecture and bricolage. *Economy and Society*, 39: 33–63.

Engelen, E., Erturk, I., Froud, J., Johal, S., Leaver, A., Moran, M. and Williams, K. (2012) Misrule of experts? The financial crisis as elite debacle. *Economy and Society*, 41: 360–382.

Euromoney (2014) Offshore renminbi: Bank of China CEO gives London edge over Luxembourg, Saigal K And Gangahar A 31 January 2014. Available at: https://www.euromoney.com/article/b12kkfm83rxc95/offshore-renminbi-bank-of-china-ceo-gives-london-edge-over-luxembourg.

Faulconbridge, J.R. (2004) London and Frankfurt in Europe's evolving financial centre network. *Area*, 36(3): 235–244.

Faulconbridge, J.R. and Hall, S. (2014) Reproducing the City of London's institutional landscape: the role of education and learning of situated practices by early career elites. *Environment and Planning A*, 46(7): 1682–1698.

Faulconbridge, J. and Muzio, D. (2009) The financialization of large law firms: situated discourses and practices of reorganization. *Journal of Economic Geography*, 9: 641–661.

Faulconbridge, J. and Muzio, D. (2015) Global professional service firms and the challenge of institutional complexity: 'field relocation' as a response strategy. *Journal of Management Studies*, 53(1): 89–124.

Folkman, P., Froud, J., Johal, S. and Williams, K. (2007) Working for themselves? Capital market intermediaries and present day capitalism. *Business History*, 49: 552–572.

Foucault, M. (1979) *Discipline and Punish: The Birth of the Prison*. New York: Vintage Books.

French, S. and Kneale, J. (2009) Excessive financialization: insuring lifestyles, enlivening subjects and everyday spaces of biosocial excess. *Environment and Planning D*, 27: 1030–1053.

French, S. and Kneale, J. (2012) Speculating on careless lives. *Journal of Cultural Economy*, 5(4): 391–406.

French, S. and Leyshon, A. (2010) These f@#king guys: the terrible waste of a good crisis. *Environment and Planning A*, 42(11): 2549–2559.

French, S., Leyshon, A. and Signoretta, P. (2008) 'All gone now': the material, discursive and political erasure of bank and building society branches in Britain. *Antipode*, 40(1): 79–101.

French, S. and Leyshon, A. (2004) The new financial system? Towards a conceptualization of financial reintermediation. *Review of International Political Economy*, 11(2): 263–288.

French, S., Leyshon, A. and Wainwright, T. (2011) Financializing space, spacing financialization. *Progress in Human Geography*, 35(6): 798–819.

Froud, J.C., Johal, S. and Williams, K.H. (2000) Shareholder value and financialization: consultancy promises and management moves. *Economy and Society*, 29(1): 90–110.

Froud, J., Haslam, C., Johal, S. and Williams, K. (2002) Cars after financialisation: a case study in financial under-performance, constraints and consequences. *Competition and Change*, 6: 13–41.

Froud, J., Johal, S., Leaver, A. and Williams, K. (2006) *Financialization and Strategy: Narrative and Numbers*. London: Routledge.

FSA (2009) The Turner Review: a regulatory response to the global banking crisis. Available at: www.fsa.gov.uk/pubs/other/turner_review.pdf, last accessed 10 April 2017

FSSC (2007) *Skills Review: UK Wholesale Financial Services*. London: Financial Services Skills Council.

Getler, M.S. (2001) Best practice? Geography, learning and the institutional limits to strong convergence. *Journal of Economic Geography*, 1(1): 5–26.

GFCI (2007) The Global Financial Centres Index, 1 March 2007. London: Z/Yen and the City of London Corporation.

GFCI (2014) The Global Financial Centres Index, 16 September 2014. London: Z/Yen and Qatar Financial Centre Authority.

Gherardi, S. (2009) Practice? It's a matter of taste! *Management Learning*, 40: 535–550.

Ghosh, S., Gonzalez del Mazo, I. and Otker-Robe, I. (2012) Chasing the shadows: how significant is shadow banking in emerging markets? *Economic Premise*, No. 88, The World Bank. Available at: http://siteresources.worldbank.org/EXTPREMNET/Resources/EP88.pdf, last accessed 25 June 2014.

Gibbon, P. (2002) At the cutting edge: financialization and UK clothing retailers' global saving patterns and practices. *Competition and Change*, 6: 289–308.

Gilbert, E. (1998) 'Ornamenting the facade of Hell': iconographies of nineteenth-century Canadian paper money. *Environment and Planning D: Society and Space*, 16: 57–80.

Grabher, G. (1993) *The Embedded Firm: On the Socioeconomics of Industrial Networks*. London: Routledge.

Guardian (2012) How much tax do Starbucks, Facebook and the biggest US companies pay in the UK? Available at: www.guardian.co.uk/news/datablog/2012/oct/16/tax-biggest-us-companies-uk, last accessed 14 December 2016.

Guardian (2016) Admiral to price car insurance based on Facebook posts. Available at: www.theguardian.com/technology/2016/nov/02/admiral-to-price-car-insurance-based-on-facebook-posts, last accessed 14 December 2016.

Haberly, D. and Wójcik, D. (2015) Regional blocks and imperial legacies: mapping the global offshore FDI network. *Economic Geography*, 91(3): 251–280.

Hadjimichalis, C. (2011) Uneven geographical development and socio-spatial justice and solidarity: European regions after the 2009 financial crisis. *European Urban and Regional Studies*, 18(3): 254–274.

Hall, S. (2006) What counts? Exploring the production of quantitative financial narratives in London's corporate finance industry. *Journal of Economic Geography*, 6(5): 661–678.

Hall, S. (2007) 'Relational marketplaces' and the rise of boutiques in London's corporate finance industry. *Environment and Planning A*, 39(8): 1838–1854.

Hall, S. (2008) Geographies of business education: MBA programmes, reflexive business schools and the cultural circuit of capital. *Transactions of the Institute of British Geographers*, 33(1): 27–41.

Hall, S. (2009) Financialized elites and the changing nature of finance capitalism: investment bankers in London's financial district. *Competition & Change*, 13(2): 175–191.

Hall, S. (2011) Geographies of money and finance I: cultural economy, politics and place. *Progress in Human Geography*, 35(2): 234–245.

Hall, S. (2012) Geographies of money and finance II: financialization and financial subjects. *Progress in Human Geography*, 36(3): 403–411.

Hall, S. (2013) Business education and the (re)production of gendered cultures of work in the City of London. *Social Politics*, 20(2): 222–241.

Hall, S. (2015) Banking with Chinese characteristics in London's financial district: state-led internationalisation and the challenge of market making. Working paper (copy available from author).

Hall, S. (2017) Rethinking international financial centres through the politics of territory: renminbi internationalisation in London's financial district. *Transactions of the Institute of British Geographers*, DOI: 10.1111/tran.12172.

Hall, S. and Appleyard, L. (2009) 'City of London, City of Learning'? Placing business education within the geographies of finance. *Journal of Economic Geography*, 9(5): 597–617.

Hall, S. and Appleyard, L. (2011) Commoditising learning: cultural economy and the growth of for-profit educational service firms in London. *Environment and Planning A*, 43(1): 10–27.

Hall, S.M. (2015) Everyday family experiences of the financial crisis: getting by in the recent economic recession. *Journal of Economic Geography*. doi: 10.1093/jeg/lbv007.

Hampton, M.P. and Abbott, J. (eds) (1999) *Offshore Finance Centres and Tax Havens*. London: Macmillan.

Hampton, M.P. and Christensen, J.E. (1999) Treasure Island revisited. Jersey's offshore finance centre crisis: implications for other small island economies. *Environment and Planning A*, 31: 1619–1637.

Hampton, M.P. and Christensen, J.E. (2002) Offshore pariahs? Small island economies, tax havens, and the re-configuration of global finance. *World Development*, 30(9): 1657–1673.

Hanlon, G. (2004) Institutional forms and organizational structures: homology, trust and reputational capital in professional service firms. *Organization*, 11: 186–210.

Harvey, D. (1982) *The Limits to Capital*. Oxford: Blackwell.

Harvey, D. (1990) Between space and time: reflections on the geographical imagination. *Annals of the Association of American Geographers*, 80: 418–434.

Harvey, D. (2010) *The Enigma Capital and the Crises of Capitalism*. London: Profile Books.

Harvey, D. (2014) *Seventeen Contradictions and the End of Capitalism*. London: Profile Books.

He, D. and McCauley, R. (2010) Offshore markets for the domestic currency: monetary and financial stability issues. *BIS Working Papers,* No. 320. Basel: Bank for International Settlements.

Helleiner, E. and Kirshner, J. (eds) (2014) *The Great Wall of Money: Power and Politics in China's International Monetary Relations.* Ithaca, NY: Cornell University Press.

Hertz, E. (1998) *The Trading Crowd: An Ethnography of the Shanghai Stock Market.* Cambridge: Cambridge University Press.

HKMA (2013) *Hong Kong: China's Global financial Centre.* Available at: http://www.fstb.gov.hk/fsb/topical/doc/pitchbook_brochure(Nov%202013)_e.pdf.

Ho, K. (2009) *Liquidated: An Ethnography of Wall Street.* Durham, NC: Duke University Press.

Huang, Y. (2014) 'Realising China's sustainable growth rate', *Financial Times,* 24 October. Available at: http://blogs.ft.com/the-a-list/2014/10/24/realising-chinas-sustainable-growth- rate/, last accessed 12 December 2014.

Huat, T.C. (1987) *Financial Markets and Institutions in Singapore.* Singapore: Singapore University Press.

Hudson, A.C. (1998) Reshaping the regulatory landscape: border skirmishes around the Bahamas and Cayman offshore financial centres. *Review of International Political Economy,* 5: 534–564.

Hudson, A.C. (2000) Offshoreness, globalization and sovereignty: a postmodern geo-political economy? *Transactions of the Institute of British Geographers,* 25: 269–283.

IMF (International Monetary Fund) (2015) IMF's Executive Board completes review of SDR basket, includes Chinese Renminbi', *IMF Press Release Publications,* 30 November. Available at: www.imf.org/external/np/sec/pr/2015/pr15540.htm, last accessed 14 December 2016.

Johannesen, M.N. (2014) Tax evasion and Swiss bank deposits. *Journal of Public Economics,* 111: 46–62.

Johnson, L. (2013) Catastrophe bonds and financial risk: securing capital and rule through contingency. *Geoforum,* 45: 30–40.

Johnson, L. (2014) Geographies of securitized catastrophe risk and the implications of climate change. *Economic Geography,* 90: 155–185.

Jones, A.M. (1998) (Re)producing gender cultures: theorizing gender in investment banking recruitment. *Geoforum,* 29: 451–474.

Jones, A. and Murphy, J.T. (2010) Practice and economic geography. *Geography compass,* 4: 303–319.

Jones, A. and Murphy, J.T. (2011) Theorizing practice in economic geography: foundations, challenges, and possibilities. *Progress in Human Geography,* 35(3): 366–392.

Khurana, R. (2010) *From Higher Aims to Hired Hands: The Social Transformation of American Business Schools and the Unfulfilled Promise of Management as a Profession.* Princeton, NJ: Princeton University Press.

Knorr Cetina, K. and Bruegger, U. (2002) Global microstructures: the virtual societies of financial markets. *American Journal of Sociology,* 107: 905–950.

Knox-Hayes, J. (2009) The developing carbon financial service industry: expertise, adaptation and complementarity in London and New York. *Journal of Economic Geography*, 9: 749–777.

Knox-Hayes, J. (2013) The spatial and temporal dynamics of value in financialisation: analysis of the infrastructure of carbon markets. *Geoforum*, 50: 117–128.

Krippner, G. (2005) The financialization of the American economy. *Socio-Economic Review*, 3: 173–208.

Kynaston, D. (2002) *The City of London Volume 4: A Club No More 1945–2000*. London: Pimlico.

Lai, K.P.Y. (2012) Differentiated markets: Shanghai, Beijing and Hong Kong in China's financial centre network. *Urban Studies*, 49(6): 1275–1296.

Lai, K.P.Y. (2016) Financial advisors, financial ecologies and the variegated financialisation of everyday investors. *Transactions of the Institute of British Geographers*, 41: 27–40.

Land Registry (2016) House Price Index for UK, January 2010 – July 2017. Available at: http://landregistry.data.gov.uk/app/ukhpi/explore, last accessed 6 October 2016.

Langley, P. (2006) Securitising suburbia: the transformation of Anglo-American mortgage finance. *Competition and Change*, 10(3): 283–299.

Langley, P. (2007) The uncertain subjects of Anglo-American financialization. *Cultural Critique*, 65: 66–91.

Langley, P. (2008) *The Everyday Life of Global Finance Saving and Borrowing in Anglo-America*. Oxford: Oxford University Press.

Langley, P. (2010) The performance of liquidity in the subprime mortgage crisis. *New Political Economy*, 15: 71–89.

Langley, P. (2014) Equipping entrepreneurs: consuming credit and credit scores. *Consumption Markets & Culture*, 17: 448–467.

Langley, P. (2016) Crowdfunding in the UK: a cultural economy. *Economic Geography*, 92(3): 301–321.

Langley, P. and Leyshon, A. (2016) Platform capitalism: the intermediation and capitalization of digital economic circulation. *Finance and Society*, 2(1): 1–21.

Larner, W. (2007) Expatriate experts and globalizing governmentalities: the New Zealand diaspora strategy. *Transactions of the Institute of British Geographers*, 32: 331–345.

Larner, W. and Walters, W. (2005) *Global Governmentality: New Perspectives on International Rule*. London: Routledge.

Lee, R. (2006) The ordinary economy: tangled up in values and geography. *Transactions of the Institute of British Geographers*, 31: 413–432.

Lewis, M. (1989) *Liar's Poker: Rising Through the Wreckage of Wall Street*. New York: W. W. Norton and Co.

Lewis, M. (2010) *The Big Short: Inside the Doomsday Machine*. London: Allen.

Leyshon, A. (1995) Geographies of financial exclusion: financial abandonment in Britain and the United States. *Transactions of the Institute of British Geographers* 20(3): 312–341.

Leyshon, A. (1998) Geographies of money and finance III. *Progress in Human Geography*, 22(3): 433–446.

Leyshon, A. and Pollard, J. (2000) Geographies of industrial convergence: the case of retail banking. *Transactions of the Institute of British Geographers*, 25(2): 203–220. doi:10.1111/j.0020-2754.2000.00203.x

Leyshon, A. and Thrift, N. (1997) *Money/Space: Geographies of Monetary Transformation*. London: Routledge.

Leyshon, A. and Thrift, N. (2007) The capitalization of almost everything: the future of finance and capitalism. *Theory, Culture and Society*, 24: 97–115.

Leyshon, A. and Tickell, A. (1994) Money order? The discursive construction of Bretton Woods and the making and breaking of regulatory space. *Environment and Planning A*, 26(12): 1861–1890.

Leyshon, A., Lee, R. and Williams, C.C. (eds) (2003) *Alternative Economic Spaces*. London: Sage.

Leyshon, A., Burton, D., Knights, D., Alferoff, C. and Signoretta, P. (2004) Towards an ecology of retail financial services: understanding the persistence of door-to-door credit and insurance providers. *Environment and Planning A*, 36(4): 625–645.

Leyshon, A., Signoretta, P., Knights, D., Alferoff, C. and Burton, D. (2006) Walking with moneylenders: the ecology of the UK home-collected credit industry. *Urban Studies*, 43(1): 161–186.

Leyshon, A., French, S. and Signoretta, P. (2008) Financial exclusion and the geography of bank and building society branch closure in Britain. *Transactions of the Institute of British Geographers*, 33(4): 447–465. doi:10.1111/j.1475-5661.2008.00323.x.

Long, J.A. and Tan, D. (2010) The growth of the private wealth management industry in Singapore and Hong Kong. *Capital Markets Law Journal*, 6: 104–126.

Lovell, H., Bebbington, J., Larrinaga, C. and Sales de Aguiar, T.R. (2013) Putting carbon markets into practice: a case study of financial accounting in Europe. *Environment and Planning C: Government and Policy*, 31(4): 741–757.

MacKenzie, D. (2003a) Long-term capital managements and the sociology of arbitrage. *Economy and Society*, 32(2): 349–380.

MacKenzie, D. (2003b) An equation and its worlds: bricolage, exemplars, disunity and performativity in financial economics. *Social Studies of Science*, 33: 831–868.

MacKenzie, D. (2006) *An Engine, Not a Camera*. Cambridge, MA: MIT Press.

MacKenzie, D. (2012) Knowledge production in financial markets: credit default swaps, the ABX and the subprime crisis. *Economy and Society*, 41: 335–359.

MacKenzie, D. (2014) Be grateful for drizzle. *London Review of Books*, 36(17): 27–30.

MacKenzie, D. and Spears, T. (2014a) 'A device for being able to book P&L': the organizational embedding of the Gaussian copula. *Social Studies of Science*, 44(3): 418–440.

MacKenzie, D. and Spears, T. (2014b) 'The formula that killed Wall Street': the Gaussian copula and modelling practices in investment banking. *Social Studies of Science*, 44(3): 393–417.

MacKenzie, D., Beunza, D., Millo, Y. and Pardo-Guerra, J.P. (2012) Drilling through the Allegheny Mountains. *Journal of Cultural Economy*, 5(3): 279–296.

MacLeavy, J. (2008) Neoliberalising subjects: the legacy of New Labour's construction of social exclusion in local governance. *Geoforum*, 39(5): 1657–1666.

MacLeavy, K. (2011) A 'new politics' of austerity, workfare and gender? The UK coalition government's welfare reform proposals. *Cambridge Journal of Regions, Economy and Society*, 4(3): 289–302.

McDowell, L. (1997) *Capital Culture*. Oxford: Blackwell.

McDowell, L. (2010) Capital culture revisited: sex, testosterone and the city. *International Journal of Urban and Regional Research*, 34(3): 652–658.

McRae, H. and Cairncross, F. (1985) *Capital City: London as a Financial Centre*. London: Methuen.

Mansfield, B. (2004) Neoliberalism in the oceans: 'rationalization', property rights, and the commons question. *Geoforum*, 35: 313–326.

Marron, D. (2007) 'Lending by numbers': credit scoring and the constitution of risk within American consumer credit. *Economy and Society*, 36: 103–133.

McDowell, L. (1997) *Capital Culture*. Oxford: Blackwell.

McDowell, L. (2010) Capital culture revisited: sex, testosterone and the city. *International Journal of Urban and Regional Research*, 34(3): 652–658.

McRae, H. and Cairncross, F. (1985) *Capital City: London as a Financial Centre*. London: Methuen.

Marshall, J.N. (2004) Financial institutions in disadvantaged areas: a comparative analysis of policies encouraging financial inclusion in Britain and the US. *Environment and Planning A*, 36: 241–261.

Marshall, J.N. (2013) A geographical political economy of banking crises: a peripheral region perspective on organisational concentration and spatial centralisation in Britain. *Cambridge Journal of Regions, Economy and Society*, 6(3): 455–477.

Marshall, J.N., Willis, R., Coombes, M., Raybould, S. and Richardson, R. (2000) Mutuality, de-mutualization and communities: the implications of branch network rationalization in the British building society industry. *Transactions of the Institute of British Geographers*, 25: 355–377.

Marshall, N., Pike, A., Pollard, J., Tomaney, J., Dawley, S. and Gray, J. (2011) Placing the run on Northern Rock. *Journal of Economic Geography*. doi: 10.1093/jeg/lbq055.

Martin, R. (ed.) (1999) *Money and the Space Economy*. Chichester: Wiley.

Martin, R. (2002) *Financialization of Everyday Life*. Philadelphia, PA: Temple University Press.

Martin, R. (2011) The local geographies of the financial crisis: from the housing bubble to economic recession. *Journal of Economic Geography*, 11(4): 587–618.

Martin, R., Pike, A., Tyler, P. and Gardiner, B. (2015) Spatially rebalancing the UK economy: the need for a new policy model. *Regional Studies Association*, pamphlet (March).

Maskell, P. (2001) The firm in economic geography. *Economic Geography*, 77: 329–344.

Maude, D. and Molyneux, P. (1996) *Private Banking*. London: Euromoney Books.

Maurer, B. (2005) *Mutual Life, Limited: Islamic Banking, Alternative Currencies, Lateral Reason*. Princeton, NJ: Princeton University Press.

Maurer, B. (2008) Re-regulating offshore finance? *Geography Compass*, 2: 155–175.

Meyer, D. (2000) *Hong Kong as a Global Metropolis*. Cambridge: Cambridge University Press.

Meyer, D.R. (2015) The world cities of Hong Kong and Singapore: network hubs of global finance. *International Journal of Comparative Sociology*, 56(3–4): 198–231.

Michie, R. (1992) *The City of London: Continuity and Change, 1850–1990*. London: Macmillan.

Mintzberg, H. (2004) *Developing Managers, not MBAs*. London: FT Prentice Hall.

Moran, M. (1991) *The Politics of the Financial Services Revolution: The USA, UK and Japan*. Basingstoke: Macmillan.

Muellerleile, C. (2009) Financialization takes off at Boeing. *Journal of Economic Geography*, 9: 663–677.

Muniesa, F., Millo, Y. and Callon, M. (2007) An introduction to market devices. *Sociological Review*, 55: 1–12.

O'Brien, P. and Pike, A. (2015) City deals, decentralisation and the governance of local infrastructure funding and financing in the UK. *National Institute Economic Review*, 233 (August): R14–R26.

O'Brien, R. (1991) *Global Financial Integration: The End of Geography*. London: Pinter.

O'Neill, P. (2001) Financial narratives of the modern corporation. *Journal of Economic Geography*, 1: 181–199.

O'Neill, P. (2009) Infrastructure investment and the management of risk. In G. Clark, A. Dixon and A. Monk (eds), *Managing Financial Risks: From Global to Local*. Oxford: Oxford University Press. pp. 165–190.

O'Neill, P. (2010) Infrastructure finance and operation in the contemporary city. *Geographical Review*, 48: 3–12.

Oxfam (2009) Working for the few. Oxfam Briefing Paper 178. Available at: www.oxfam.org/en/policy/working-for-the-few-economic-inequality, last accessed 25 June 2014.

Pacione, M. (2005) Dubai. *Cities*, 22(3): 255–265.

Palan, R. (1998) Trying to have your cake and eat it: how and why the state system has created offshore. *International Studies Quarterly*, 42: 625–643.

Palan, R. (2006) *The Offshore World: Sovereign Markets, Virtual Places and Nomad Millionaires*. Ithaca, NY: Cornell University Press.

Palan, R. and Nesvetailova, A. (2014) Elsewhere, ideally nowhere: shadow banking and offshore finance. *Politik*, 16: 26–34.

Palan, R., Murphy, R. and Chavagneux, C. (2010) *Tax Havens: How Globalization Really Works*. Ithaca, NY: Cornell University Press.

Park, Y.S. (1982) The economics of offshore financial centres. *Columbia Journal of World Business*, 17: 31–35.

Peck, J. and Tickell, A. (2002) Neoliberalizing space. *Antipode,* 34: 380–404.

People's Bank of China Study Group (2006) The timing, path and strategies of RMB internationalization. *China Finance*, 5: 12–13.

Pferrer, F. and Fong, C. (2004) The end of business schools? Less success than meets the eye. *Academy of Management, Learning and Education*, 1: 78–95.

Pike, A. (2006) 'Shareholder value' versus the regions: the closure of the Vaux Brewery in Sunderland. *Journal of Economic Geography*, 6: 201–222.

Pike, A. and Pollard, J. (2010) Economic geographies of financialization. *Economic Geography*, 86: 29–51.

Piketty, T. (2013) *Capital in the Twenty First Century*. Cambridge, MA: Belknap Press.

Piketty, T. and Saez, E. (2014) Inequality in the long-run. *Science*, 344: 838–842.

Pollard, J. (2003) Small firm finance and economic geography. *Journal of Economic Geography*, 3: 429–452.

Pollard, J. and Samers, M. (2007) Islamic banking and finance: postcolonial political economy and the decentring of economic geography. *Transactions of the Institute of British Geographers*, 32(3): 313–330.

Pollard, J. and Samers, M. (2013) Governing Islamic finance: territory, agency, and the making of cosmopolitan financial geographies. *Annals of the Association of American Geographers*, 103(3): 710–726.

Pollard, J., Oldfield, J., Randalls, S. and Thornes, J. (2008) Firm finances, weather derivatives and geography. *Geoforum*, 39: 616–624.

Pollard, J., McEwan, C., Laurie, N. and Stenning, A. (2009) Economic geography under postcolonial scrutiny. *Transactions of the Institute of British Geographers*, 34(2): 137–142.

Pryke, M. (1991) An international city going global: spatial change in the City of London. *Environment and Planning D: Society and Space*, 9: 197–222.

Pryke, M. (2006) Making finance, making worlds. In N. Clark, D. Massey and P. Sarre (eds), *A World in the Making*. Milton Keynes: Open University Press.

Pryke, M. and Allen, J. (2000) Monetized time-space: derivatives – money's new imaginary. *Economy and Society*, 2: 264–284.

Pryke, M. and Du Gay, P. (2007) Take an issue: cultural economy and finance. *Economy and Society*, 36(3): 339–354.

PwC (2015) The long awaited Renminbi Qualified Foreign Institutional Investor (RQFII) quota granted to Luxembourg. Available at: www.pwc.lu/en/china/docs/pwc-china-290415.pdf, last accessed 3 August 2015.

Reckwitz, A. (2002) Toward a theory of social practices: a development in culturalist theorizing. *European Journal of Social Theory*, 5: 243–263.

Reuters (2015) Beijing's stock rescue has $800 billion bark, small market bite, 23 July. Available at: http://uk.reuters.com/article/uk-china-markets-rescue-idUKK CN0PX0AU20150723, last accessed 14 December 2016.

Rixen, T. (2013) Why regulation after the crisis is feeble: shadow banking, offshore financial centres and jurisdictional competition. *Regulation and Governance*, 7: 435–459.

Roberts, R. and Kynaston, D. (2001) *City State: How Markets Came to Rule Our World*. London: Profile Books.

Roberts, S.M. (1994) Fictitious capital, fictitious spaces: the geography of offshore financial flows. In S. Corbridge, R. Martin and N. Thrift (eds), *Money, Power and Space*. Oxford: Blackwell. pp. 91–115.

Roberts, S.M. (1995) Small place, big money: the Cayman Islands and the international financial system. *Economic Geography*, 71: 237–256.

Røpke, I. (2009) Theories of practice – new inspiration for ecological economic studies on consumption. *Ecological Economics*, 68: 2490–2497.

Rowlingson, K. and McKay, S. (2015) Financial Inclusion: Annual Monitoring Report. University of Birmingham and Friends Provident Foundation.

Sarre, P. (2007) Understanding the geography of international finance. *Geography Compass*, 1: 1076–1096.

Sassen, S. (2001 [1991]) *The Global City*. Princeton, NJ: Princeton University Press.

Sassen, S. (2012) *Cities in a World Economy*, 4th edition. London: Sage.

Savage, M. and Williams, K. (eds) (2008) *Remembering Elites*. Oxford: Blackwell.

Saxenian, A. (1994) *Regional Advantage: Culture and Competition in Silicon Valley and Route 128*. Cambridge, MA: Harvard University Press.

Schenk, C. (1998) The origins of the Eurodollar markets in London: 1955–1963. *Explorations in Economic History*, 35: 221–238.

Seabrooke, L. and Wigan, D. (2014) Global wealth chains in the international political economy. *Review of International Political Economy*, 21: 257–263.

Shaxson, N. (2012) *Treasure Islands: Tax Havens and the Men Who Stole the World*. London: Vintage, Random House.

Shaxson, N. and Christensen, J. (2013) The finance curse: How oversized financial centres attack democracies and corrupt economies. Tax Justice Network. Available at: http://www.taxjustice.net/topics/finance-sector/finance-curse/.

Sheller, M. and Urry, J. (2006) The new mobilities paradigm. *Environment and Planning A*, 38(2): 207–226. doi:10.1068/a37268

Short, J.R. (2013) Economic wealth and political power in the second Gilded Age. In I. Hay (ed.), *Geographies of the Super-Rich*. Cheltenham: Edward Elgar. pp. 25-43.

Shove, E. (2003) *Comfort, Cleanliness and Convenience: The Social Organization of Normality*. Oxford: Berg.

Shove, E., Pantzar, M. and Watson, M. (2012) *The Dynamics of Social Practice: Everyday Life and How It Changes*. London: Sage.

Sidaway, J. (2008) Subprime crisis: American crisis or human crisis? *Environment and Planning D: Society and Space*, 26: 195–198.

Sikka, P. (2003) The role of offshore financial centres in globalization. *Accounting Forum*, 27: 365–399.

Sikka, P. and Willmott, H. (2010) The dark side of transfer pricing: its role in tax avoidance and wealthy retentiveness. *Critical Perspectives on Accounting*, 21: 342–356.

Sklair, L. (2001) *The Transnational Capitalist Class*. Oxford: Blackwell.

Spiegelberg, R. (1973) *The City: Power Without Accountability*. London: Bland and Briggs.

Starkey, K., Hatchuel, A. and Tempest, S. (2004) Rethinking the business school. *Journal of Management Studies*, 41: 1521–1531.

Storper, M. (2011) Why do regions develop and change? The challenge for geography and economics. *Journal of Economic Geography*, 11: 333–346.

Strange, S. (1986) *Casino Capitalism*. Manchester: Manchester University Press.

Strange, S. (1998) *Mad Money*. Manchester: Manchester University Press.

Tax Justice Network (2005) The price of offshore revisited. Available at: www.taxjustice.net/cms/upload/pdf/Price_of_Offshore_Revisited_120722.pdf, last accessed 25 June 2014.

Tax Justice Network (2012) New estimates for 'missing' global private wealth, income, inequality and lost taxes. www.taxjustice.net/cms/upload/pdf/Price_of_Offshore_Revisited_120722.pdf, last accessed 10 April 2017.

Taylor, P.J. (2001) Regionality within globalization: what does it mean for Europe? In F.M. Zimmerman and S. Janschitz (eds), *Regional Policies in Europe: Key Opportunities for Regions in the 21st Century*. Graz: Leykam. pp. 49–64.

Taylor, P.J. (2006) Shanghai, Hong Kong, Taipei and Beijing within the World City Netowrk: Positions, tends and Prospects. GaWC Research Bulletin 204. Available at: www.lboro.ac.uk/gawc.

Tett, G. (2009) *Fool's Gold: How Unrestrained Greed Corrupted a Dream, Shattered Global Markets and Unleashed a Catastrophe*. London: Little, Brown.

TheCityUK (2015) *Key Facts about UK Financial and Related Professional Services*. London: TheCityUK.

Thrift, N. (1994) On the social and cultural determinants of international financial centres: the case of the City of London. In N. Thrift, S. Corbridge and R. Martin (eds), *Money, Power and Space*. Oxford: Blackwell.

Thrift, N. (2005) *Knowing Capitalism*. London: Sage.

Thrift, N. and Olds, K. (2004) Cultures on the brink: reengineering the soul of capitalism – on a global scale. In A. Ong and S.J.Collier (eds), *Global Assemblages: Technology Politics and Ethics as Anthropological Problems*. Malden, MA; Oxford: Blackwell.

Tickell, A. (1994) Banking on Britain? The changing role and geography of Japanese banks in Britain. *Regional Studies*, 28(3): 291–304.

Tickell, A. (1996) Making a melodrama out of a crisis: reinventing the collapse of Barings Bank. *Environment and Planning D: Society and Space*, 14(1): 5–33.

Treasury Committee (2010) Women in the City, Tenth Report of Session 2009–10. House of Commons, London HC 482.

Urry, J. (2014) *Offshoring*. Cambridge: Polity.

Vickers Report (2013) *The Independent Commission on Banking: The Vickers Report*. London: Independent Commission on Banking.

Vogel, S. (1996) *Freer Markets, More Rules: Regulatory Reform in Advanced Industrial Countries*. Ithaca and London: Cornell University Press.

Wainwright, T. (2009) Laying the foundations for a crisis: mapping the historico-geographical construction of residential mortgage-backed securitization in the UK. *International Journal of Urban and Regional Research*, 33(2): 372–388.

Wainwright, T. (2011) Tax doesn't have to be taxing: London's 'onshore' finance industry and the fiscal spaces of a global crisis. *Environmental and Planning A*, 43(6): 1287–1304.

Wainwright, T. (2015) Circulating financial innovation: new knowledge and securitization in Europe. *Environment and Planning A*, 47: 1643–1660.

Walter, E.C. and Howie, F. (2011) *Red Capitalism: The Fragile Financial Foundation of China's Extraordinary Rise*. Singapore: Wiley.

Warf, B. (2002) Tailored for Panama: offshore banking at the crossroads for the Americas. *Geografiska Annaler B*, 84: 47–61.

Wenger, E. (1998) *Communities of Practice: Learning Meaning and Identity*. Cambridge: Cambridge University Press.

Whitehead, C. and Williams, P. (2011) Causes and consequences? Exploring the shape and direction of the housing system in the UK post the financial crisis. *Housing Studies*, 26(7–8): 1157–1169.

Wilk, R. (2002) Consumption, human needs, and global environmental change. *Global Environmental Change*, 12: 5–13.

Wójcik, D. (2007) Geography and the future of stock exchanges: between real and virtual space. *Growth and Change*, 38(2): 200–223.

Wójcik, D. (2009) Geography, stupid! A note on the credit crunch. *Environment and Planning A*, 41: 258–260.

Wójcik, D. (2011) Securitization and its footprint: the rise of the US securities industry centres 1990–2007. *Journal of Economic Geography*, 11: 925–947.

Wójcik, D. (2012) The end of investment bank capitalism? An economic geography of financial jobs and power. *Economic Geography*, 88(4): 345–368.

Wójcik, D. (2013) Where governance fails: advanced business services and the offshore world. *Progress in Human Geography*, 37(3): 330–347.

Wójcik, D. and Camilleri, J. (2015) 'Capitalist tools in socialist hands'? China Mobile in the global financial network. *Transactions of the Institute of British Geographers* 40(4): 464–478.

Wolfe, T. (1987) *Bonfire of the Vanities*. New York: Farrar, Straus & Giroux.

Wu, F. (2000) The global and local dimensions of place-making: remaking Shanghai as a world city. *Urban Studies*, 37(8): 1359–1377.

Wyly, E.K., Atia, M., Foxcroft, H., Hamme, D.J. and Phillips-Watts, K. (2006) American home: predatory mortgage capital and neighbourhood spaces of race and class exploitation in the United States. *Geografiska Annaler, Series B: Human Geography*, 88(1): 105–132.

Wyly, E.K., Atia, M., Lee, E. and Mendez, P. (2007) Race, gender, and statistical Representation: predatory mortgage lending and the US Community Reinvestment Movement. *Environment and Planning A*, 39: 2139–2166.

Wyly, E.K., Moos, M., Hammel, D. and Kabahizi, E. (2009) Cartographies of race and class: Mapping the class-monopoly rents of American subprime mortgage capital. *International Journal of Urban and Regional Research*, 33(2): 332–354.

Yeung, H.W. (2005) Rethinking relational economic geography. *Transactions of the Institute of British Geographers*, 30(1): 37–51.

Yeung, H.W. and Lin, G.C.S. (2003) Theorizing economic geographies of Asia. *Economic Geography*, 79(2): 107–128.

Yusuf, S. and Wu, W. (2002) Pathways to a world city: Shanghai rising in an era of globalisation. *Urban Studies*, 39(7): 1213–1240.

Zald, M.N. and Lounsbury, M. (2010) The wizards of Oz: towards an institutional approach to elites, expertise and command posts. *Organization Studies*, 31: 963–996.

Zaloom, C. (2006) *Out of the Pits: Traders and Technology from Chicago to London*. Chicago: Chicago University Press.

Zelizer, V. (1994) *The Social Meaning of Money*. New York: Basic Books.

Zhang, M. (2009) China's new international financial strategy and the global financial crisis. *China and World Economy*, 17: 22–35.

Zhang, Z., Collins, L., and Baeck, P. (2014) Understanding Alternative finance: The UK Alternative Finance Industry Report. Nesta. Available at: https://www.nesta.org.uk/sites/default/files/understanding-alternative-finance-2014.pdf.

Zhao, S.X.B. (2003) Spatial restructuring of financial centers in mainland China and Hong Kong: a geography of finance perspective. *Urban Affairs Review*, 38(4): 535–571.

Zucman, G. (2013) The missing wealth of nations: are Europe and the US net debtors or net creditors? *Quarterly Journal of Economics*, 128: 1321–1364.

Zweig, D. (2006) Competing for talent: China's strategies for reverse the brain drain. *International Labour Review*, 145: 65–90.

Z/Yen (2014) *The Global Financial Centres Index 15*. London: Z/Yen.

Z/Yen (2015) *The Global Financial Centres Index 17*. London: Z/Yen.

INDEX